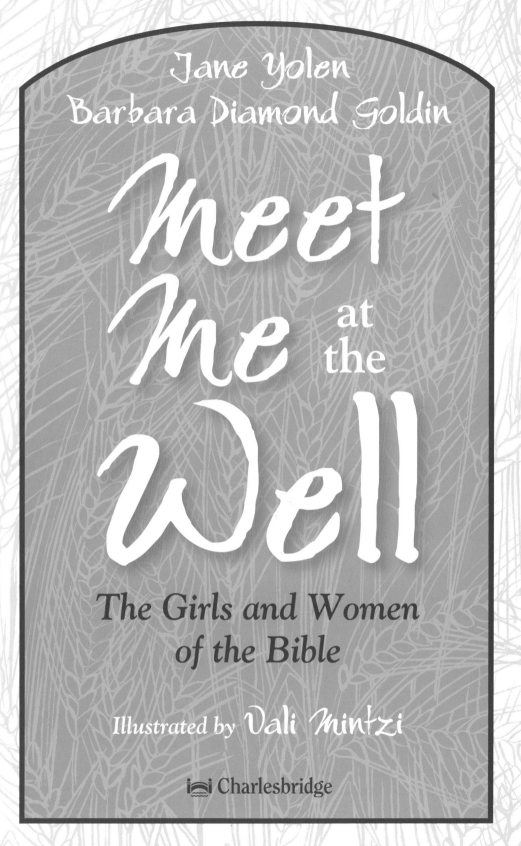

Jane Yolen
Barbara Diamond Goldin

Meet Me at the Well

The Girls and Women of the Bible

Illustrated by Vali Mintzi

ini Charlesbridge

To my daughter and five granddaughters—J. Y.

In memory of my grandmothers, Rose and Sarah—B. D. G.

To my three daughters, Alma, Ruth & Ada—V. M.

Special thanks to Rabbi Saul Perlmutter and Shoshana Zonderman, who read an earlier version of this book in manuscript form with great care and gave us very helpful feedback and advice.

The section near the end of each chapter with "Imagine" in the title is by Barbara Diamond Goldin. The poem at the end of each chapter is by Jane Yolen. The rest of the text was written or retold by both authors together.

Published by Charlesbridge
85 Main Street
Watertown, MA 02472
(617) 926-0329
www.charlesbridge.com

Library of Congress Cataloging-in-Publication Data
Names: Yolen, Jane, author. | Goldin, Barbara Diamond, author. | Mintzi, Vali, illustrator.
Title: Meet me at the well: the girls and women of the Bible / Jane Yolen and Barbara Diamond Goldin;
illustrated by Vali Mintzi.
Description: Watertown, MA: Charlesbridge, [2017]
Identifiers: LCCN 2016053962 (print) | LCCN 2016056398 (ebook) |
ISBN 9781580893749 (reinforced for library use) | ISBN 9781607349273 (ebook) |
ISBN 9781607346463 (ebook pdf)
Subjects: LCSH: Women in the Bible. | Bible. Old Testament—Criticism, interpretation, etc.
Classification: LCC BS1199.W7 Y65 2017 (print) | LCC BS1199.W7 (ebook) | DDC
221.9/22082—dc23
LC record available at https://lccn.loc.gov/2016053962

Printed in China
(hc) 10 9 8 7 6 5 4 3 2 1

Color illustrations done in Gouache on Sennelier 300g/m2, acid free, watercolor paper
Backgrounds done in black ink on Strathmore 300g/m2, acid free, watercolor paper
Display type set in Xan by t Wiescher, Autographis
Text type set in Adobe Jenson Pro by Adobe Systems Incorporated
Color separations by Colourscan Print Co Pte Ltd, Singapore
Printed by 1010 Printing International Limited in Huizhou, Guangdong, China
Production supervision by Brian G. Walker
Designed by Diane M. Earley

Contents

Note: We have condensed each biblical account. If you want to read the extended story, use your own Bible, borrow one from a library, or find one on the Internet.

A Note from the Authors

In this book, when we refer to the Bible, we mean the Hebrew Bible, also known as the Torah, the Pentateuch, or the Old Testament (as it's often referred to outside of the Jewish community). Many of the girls and women in the Hebrew Bible are strong-willed and tough-minded and demonstrate faith, daring, and endurance. They are also resourceful, courageous, inventive, and smart. These biblical women range from Eve, first woman and first mother; to Deborah, who was a war leader, prophet, and judge in Israel; to Queen Esther, who saved her people.

There are, of course, many other women in the Bible who play smaller roles—women such as Rahav (Rachav), who helped Jewish scouts escape, and the Queen of Sheba, who ran her own country. Many unnamed women can be found in the Bible, too: Noah's wife; the mother of the Maccabees; and Zelophehad's five daughters, who, because he had no sons to inherit his land and valuables, helped change inheritance laws. There are also stories in the Bible about "bad" women—wicked queens, spies, seductresses, and courtesans—but this is not a book about them.

Biblical stories often seem to be all about the men. Remember that in biblical times, Israelite society was a patriarchy, which means that almost everything was ruled, owned, and run by men. Land and family riches were handed down from father to son with

> ### WHAT IS THE TORAH?
> *The Hebrew Bible, called the Old Testament outside of the Jewish community, includes the five books of Moses: Genesis, Exodus, Leviticus, Numbers, and Deuteronomy. The most well-known stories come from Genesis and Exodus. Some Jewish people use the term Tanakh to refer to the whole Hebrew Bible, including the books The Prophets and The Writings. Other people use the word Torah to mean all Jewish sacred literature.*

Meet Me at the Well

only a few exceptions. Almost all the charismatic leaders (called judges at that time), prophets who led the people through tangles of moral issues, heads of tribes, kings, generals, soldiers, and priests were men.

Still we must never forget that even in the stories about men, there are women. They are mothers, daughters, sisters, wives. They do a lot of the hard lifting, listening, and reacting. Most often they are part of their father's or husband's or son's narratives, so we must do double-duty in order to both situate the women in and then liberate them from the tellings.

Remember, too, that Bible stories aren't like modern novels, full of character development, dialogue that moves the story along, and a plot we can recognize. These stories are bare-boned, essentials only, and written for an audience who was used to this kind of storytelling. We won't see rounded main characters and a reasonable cause and effect in the stories. Finding the cause and effect is left to the reader. These are stories that run both with and counter to history. They make us ask questions, tease out meanings, and find the missing pieces for ourselves as the rabbis and other readers have done for centuries.

We have chosen to retell the stories of fourteen strong biblical women. In each story we begin with a brief overview of the woman (or women) involved, giving the reader a snapshot of who she is and how she fits into history and culture. We attempt to answer

---

WHAT IS MIDRASH?

The word midrash *actually means to search out or examine. Sometimes a* midrash *expands on a biblical story; sometimes it comments on elements of the story—a character's motives or the various meanings of a word. Classical* midrashim *refer to written or oral works from hundreds and even thousands of years ago in which rabbis discussed laws and passages in the Torah. Today some people extend the term and define it as a Jewish story that explains, clarifies, or elaborates on an event or passage in the Bible, often suggesting how the passage may relate to everyday life.*

---

the question: What makes this woman a hero of this tale? We then condense the Bible story to concentrate on the woman's role. If you want to know the larger, longer, and more detailed story, you can use your own Bible, borrow one from a library, or find one on the Internet.

In this book we refer to the women by their English names, and we provide their Hebrew names in parentheses. Alongside each story you will find sidebars containing information, commentaries, folklore, cultural annotations, and historical notes. We decided to carry on the tradition of marginalia as it is used in Jewish texts such as the Talmud and in some Passover Haggadot. The sidebars ask and answer questions we think might come up for readers because we asked ourselves the same questions while writing this book.

Rabbis and religious leaders from other traditions from ancient times forward have wrestled with Bible stories, thinking and writing about what they mean, the relevance of their cultural context, and how they support beliefs and laws. This type of commentary or musing about the Bible is called *midrash* in Hebrew. The plural is *midrashim*. Some *midrashim* in this book come from rabbis through the long centuries. Others come from more recent readings of the Bible, including those from a feminist perspective. And some are born of our own original research and responses.

Our book also includes original poems and a section in each chapter that attempts to go deeper inside each woman's thoughts—to "imagine" her. We hope to help readers meet, re-meet, and re-imagine these fourteen wonderful women of the Bible.

As we worked on this book, we came to realize that the two of us have very different approaches to biblical text. Barbara tends to stick more closely to the strict meaning of the verses, and Jane comes to them with more of a storyteller's eye. We think this is because we came from very different religious backgrounds. While Barbara

meet me at the well

was raised in a Conservative Jewish household, Jane grew up in a Reform family.

Although most of the commentary in this book is from Jewish sources, we have also included bits from other faiths, specifically Christianity and Islam, since the people, places, and stories here are common to all three religions.

As to the title—why did we choose *Meet Me at the Well?* You will discover that often the well—a source of good water in a desert world—is the meeting place where teenage girls discover their future husbands, women meet to exchange gossip and news, and animals are watered. Plus, when the Israelites trekked in the endless desert for forty years, the person who brought along a portable well gifted by God was Miriam. And for that she has been remembered and memorialized by Jews for all time.

We were often surprised by how readings from *midrash*, modern feminist commentaries, anthropological studies, and other works helped us see the Bible stories anew. While some of what we read might have at first appeared old, irrelevant, or inexplicable, a lot became fresh and stunning in our eyes as we contemplated meanings in new and different ways.

We invite you to enjoy in joy. Learn something new, and revel in these fascinating women. The whole book you hold in your hands is our *midrash*. Don't forget: while you read, ask your own questions and write your own *midrash*—even adding them (unless this is a library book!) in the margins.

Eve

First Woman, First Garden

Whether one believes *literally in the story of Eve as the history of how God made the first man and woman in the world or reads it as a folktale, parable, or creation metaphor, it's a marvelous tale. Eve is curious, daring, and courageous. As for the story itself, it's not just about beginnings. It's also about conscience, obedience, self-will, and the difficulties and glories that knowledge can bring.*

Eve appears in the Bible in the Book of Genesis, chapters and verses 1:26–27, 2:5–25, 3:1–23, 4:1–2, and 4:25.

There are two tellings in the Book of Genesis about the creation of Adam and Eve. In the first, God creates Adam and Eve simultaneously on the sixth day. In the second God creates Adam, and almost as an afterthought, God makes Eve from Adam's rib to be Adam's helper, partner, helpmeet, and wife. Many scholars believe that the second story is the same as the first, just told in greater detail.

The First Story of Adam and Eve

On the sixth day of Creation, God says, "Let Us make a human in Our image, after Our likeness. The human shall rule over the fish of the sea, the birds of the sky, over the animals, and all the earth, and over everything that creeps on the ground." And God creates a human in God's image—male and female God creates them.

The Second Story of Adam and Eve

God forms a human (Adam) from the dust of the earth (adamah) and blows the spirit of life into his nostrils. Thus man becomes a living being.

God then plants a garden eastward in Eden and places the human there to tend the garden and look after it. God causes every tree that is pleasant to see and good to eat to grow there. In the middle of this garden are the Tree of Life and the Tree of Knowledge of Good and Evil.

God commands the man, "Of every

WHY ARE THERE TWO STORIES OF CREATION?

"In ancient times, two rival creation myths vied for our people's allegiance. So popular were both versions of this story that when Genesis was being edited, the Torah had no choice but to include them both" (Frankel, Five Books, p. 4).

In fact many biblical scholars are convinced that the two stories were set down several centuries apart. And many people believe that both stories are the actual word of God.

tree in the Garden you may eat, but from the Tree of Knowledge of Good and Evil you must not eat, for on the day that you eat of it, you shall surely die."

After this warning, God says, "It is not good for man to be alone. I will make a helper for him."

So God causes the man to fall into a deep sleep. And God takes one of the man's ribs and fills in flesh in its place. Then God fashions the side of the man into a woman and brings her to the man.

The man says, "This one is bone of my bones and flesh of my flesh. She is called woman (*eesha*) because she was taken from man (*eesh*)." This is why a man leaves his father and mother and clings to his wife, and they shall be one flesh.

The man and the woman are both naked, and they are not ashamed.

Now, the serpent is the most cunning of any beast of the field that God had made. The serpent says to the woman, "Did God say you shall not eat of any tree in the garden?"

The woman answers, "We may eat the fruit of any tree, but not the tree in the center. God said, 'You shall neither eat of it nor touch it, lest you die.'"

The serpent says, "You will not die. God told you that because if you eat the fruit of the tree in the center of the garden, then your eyes will be opened and you will be like God. You will know good and evil."

The woman sees that the tree is good for eating and a means to obtaining wisdom. She takes its fruit and eats,

---

IS THE WOMAN (EVE) REALLY MADE FROM THE MAN'S (ADAM'S) RIB?

Probably not. The Etz Hayim commentary says, "The rib here connotes a physical link and signifies the partnership and companionship of male and female" (Lieber, p. 16). The Hebrew word tsela *appears in the Book of Genesis and is sometimes translated as "rib," sometimes as "side," and sometimes mistranslated as "tail." Since written Hebrew has no vowels, sometimes a single word can be read as having several very different meanings.*

---

and gives it to her husband who is with her, and he eats. Then both their eyes are opened. They realize they are naked. They sew together a fig leaf and make themselves a covering.

The man and the woman hear the sound of God in the garden and hide among the trees. God calls out to the man, "Where are you?"

"I heard You, and I was afraid because I am naked, so I hid," says the man.

"Who told you that you are naked?" says God. "Did you eat from the tree of which I forbade you to eat?"

And the man says, "The woman whom You gave to be with me—she gave me of the tree, and I ate."

"What have you done?" God says to the woman.

"The serpent deceived me, and I ate," she answers.

And God tells the serpent, "Because you did this, you shall be more cursed than all the beasts of the field. You shall crawl upon your belly and eat dust all the days of your life. You and the woman shall be enemies and so, too, your offspring and hers. They shall strike at your head, and you will bite their heel."

WAS THE FRUIT AN APPLE?

In the Hebrew text no specific fruit is mentioned. Early rabbis have commented that the fruit was possibly a fig, grapes, a citron (a lemon-like fruit), or a pomegranate, all of which are found in the Middle East. The apple was introduced later in Christian translations.

To the woman, God says, "I will increase your pain during childbirth, and your husband shall rule over you."

To Adam, God says, "Because you listened to your wife's voice and ate from the tree which I told you not to eat from, cursed is the ground because of you. Thorns and thistles shall it sprout for you. Your food will be the grasses of the field. You shall eat only by the sweat of your brow until you return to the ground from which you were taken. For you are dust, and to dust shall you return."

Then the man calls his wife Eve (Havvah in Hebrew, which could mean "living thing" or "propagator of life"), because she is the mother of all the living. And God makes Adam and Eve garments of animal skin to clothe them.

God says, "Man has become like one of Us, knowing good and evil." So that Adam and Eve don't also eat from the Tree of Life, which would cause them to live forever, God banishes them from Eden to work the soil from which man was formed. God stations the winged cherubim at the east of the Garden of Eden and the flame of the ever-turning sword to guard the way to the Tree of Life.

> ### IS THE SNAKE REALLY EVIL?
> In the ancient cultures surrounding the Israelites, the serpent was often considered a symbol of potency and rebirth—something positive. But in Western traditions the serpent is thought of as venomous, tricky, and vile. In the Islamic Qur'an the snake is not the evil seducer. It is Satan himself who convinces Adam and Eve to eat the forbidden fruit.

How Does the Eden Story Present Good and Evil?

Judaism doesn't include the idea of original sin, the belief that because Adam and Eve ate the forbidden fruit, all babies thereafter are born in sin. That idea developed with Christianity in the second century. Instead, rabbis discuss the idea of the evil impulse (yetzer ha'rah) and the good impulse (yetzer ha'tov). The more closely people adhere to the commandments, the more likely people are to make wise decisions. In Christianity the eating of the fruit is considered the "fall of man," a phrase that isn't found in the Hebrew Bible or Jewish literature (Plaut, p. 38).

Where Was Eden?

Some researchers believe that the original Garden of Eden was in Mesopotamia (now called Iraq), where the Tigris and Euphrates Rivers meet, or in the Persian Gulf. Others believe it was in Mongolia or Ethiopia or India, or even in the Americas before the continents drifted apart. Still others think that Eden was situated on the lost island of Atlantis. Some Bible scholars insist that this is a story to teach a lesson about obedience, defiance, and choice, as well as about humanity's relationship to God, and that Eden was not meant as a real place.

A Tale About a Thief

A Roman once said to Rabbi Eliezer's wife, "Your God is nothing but a thief. In your own Torah it says God caused Adam to fall asleep and only then did God take one of his ribs to form Eve."

The rabbi's wife ignored the Roman and instead called for the guard. "Help, help!" she cried. Worried, the Roman asked, "What is wrong?"

She looked at him and said, "Last night thieves visited us. They took our silver pitcher and left a gold one in its place."

The Roman laughed. "I wish a thief like that would visit me."

The rabbi's wife smiled. "That is exactly what happened to Adam. God took a rib from him and left him a valuable gift instead—his wife" (Shachter, p. 39a).

meet me at the well

RETELLING THE FOLKTALE OF LILITH, ADAM'S WIFE BEFORE EVE

The origin of this tale is from the biblical phrase "male and female God created them," which is from the first story of Adam and Eve in Genesis. Some biblical scholars comment that because there were two stories of Creation, then that means there were two different wives. One wife was created at the same time as Adam, the other from his rib. They point out that Adam and Eve aren't named in the first story but are called "man" and "woman." This is a shortened version with additional information:

When Adam viewed the animals and named them, he saw that none of them could be a partner for him, and he felt alone. So God created a partner out of the dust of the earth, just as Adam had been created. Her name was Lilith, but she was with Adam for only a short time because she insisted on full equality with him in all ways. They fought about it constantly.

Seeing no end to their quarreling, Lilith pronounced God's name and by the power the name conferred, she vanished to the Red Sea, where she lived in a cave with demons. There she was the Queen of Demons and had many demon babies.

Adam once again felt alone, though this time his complaint was that his wife had left. So God sent three angels to bring her back— Senoy, Sansenoy, and Semangelof. They told Lilith that if she didn't return, one hundred of her demon children would die every day.

Lilith refused and from that day on, she has been called both a demon and a witch, taking her revenge by killing human infants, flying above their cradles, her great wings flapping and long black hair in tangles. Of course this is only a tale, a superstition. Still, some cautious parents have warded off evil by hanging an amulet inscribed with the names of the three angels above the infant's bed or by putting an amulet around the child's neck on a chain. Even now, there are some Jewish parents who hang such amulets in a new baby's room.

Some modern women have reclaimed Lilith's power, saying that her call for equality is theirs, too. The most important feminist Jewish magazine is called Lilith. There are a number of modern reworkings of the Lilith story. Judith Plaskow's is about sisterhood and a time when Eve and Lilith meet and bond, causing God to reconsider the statement from Exodus 3:14. God tells Moses, "I am who I am . . ." but changes it to a more feminist way of thinking: "I am who I am," thought God, "but I must become who I will become."

Imagine Eve

I come here once a year, as near to this gate with its singing sword as I'm allowed. I come on the anniversary of our banishment, mine and Adam's.

I stand near the Garden and remember what it is like to be inside. In the breeze, I can smell its flowers—so many kinds—roses, oleander, lilacs, lavender, and sweet woodruff. I can hear the brooks run and see birds fly. I can even see them circle above the Garden. The music of this place is like no other. Even the trees sing in there.

I was an innocent living in the Garden. That serpent and that bite of fruit taught me many things, about my choices and their consequences, about temptation and betrayal, about fear and caution.

Our lives were simpler in the Garden. We knew only beauty. We had all we needed at our feet: food, water, love. Our lives outside the Garden are still full of the beauty of God's world. But now we have to dig for our food and find streams or wells for our water. And we must be careful to nourish our love, too, to not be so angry with each other that we destroy it.

We must be watchful for the unexpected now—a freak storm that swells the stream near our tent or lions that come down from the hills hungry for food. We traded immortality and comfort for knowledge and choice. And now we use that knowledge to care for ourselves in the world outside Paradise.

Some choices are reversible. Some are not. I still do not always know which is which. But I am more cautious now than when I was young. And I no longer listen to serpents.

Rib Woman

Rib woman, wife of dust,
who learned of apples,
serpents, lust.
With one small bite,
a rip of skin,
eternity lost,
knowledge slipped in.
A modest exchange,
a world new-made,
considering all,
a rather fair trade.

2

Sarah

The Mother of All Jews

A great beauty and a prophetess, too, Sarah is called Mother of the Jewish Nation. Yet for her first ninety-some years, she is barren—unable to bear children. Her life is filled with adventures and an almost-tragedy, and she isn't perfect by any means. Sarah's treatment of her handmaiden, Hagar (who was called the Mother of the Arabic Nations), is anything but benevolent. Yet she has God's favor, which serves her well in the end.

Sarah, the first of the four matriarchs,
is important in the Bible in the Book
of Genesis, chapters and verses
11:29–31, 12:1–20, 16:1–16,
17:1–22, 18:1–15, 20:1–18,
21:1–21, 22:1–19,
and 23:1–19.

od says to Abraham: *Lech lecha*, or Go forth, from your native land to the land that I will show you. And so Abram (Avram), as he was then called, must leave his land and his relatives and go on a journey with his wife Sarai (Saray), as she was then known, to a new place.

God promises, "I will make of you a great nation. I will bless you, and make your name great, and you shall be a blessing."

And so Abram takes Sarai and Lot, Abram's brother's son, with all their belongings and all the people who had come to them to learn about the One God, and they travel from Haran (in ancient Mesopotamia) to the land of Canaan.

Coming into Canaan they see the famine there and decide to continue into Egypt, where they hope to find food. Abram worries that because Sarai is so beautiful, his life might be in danger in Egypt if another man wants Sarai enough to kill him. So he tells Sarai, "Please say that you are my sister."

In Egypt the Egyptians do notice Sarai's great beauty, and she is taken into Pharaoh's palace. Abram is treated well because of Sarai, and he prospers. But God sends a series of plagues onto Pharaoh's household because he has taken Sarai. Pharaoh asks Abram, "Why have you done this to me? Why didn't you tell me she is your wife? Take her and go."

For years and years Sarai is barren and cannot conceive a child. At last she is much too old to ever have a baby. As was the custom of the time, in order that her husband would not remain

ARE ALL JEWS ACTUAL DESCENDANTS OF ABRAM (ABRAHAM) AND SARAI (SARAH)?

Not really. But the Torah calls Sarah and Abraham the Mother and Father of Nations. And converts to Judaism are also considered their spiritual descendants (Scherman, p. 73; Steinsaltz, p. 27).

IS SARAH MORE THAN JUST A GREAT BEAUTY?

Yes. It is said in Exodus Rabbah and Genesis Rabbah, the extensive books of midrashim, *that Sarah's gift of prophecy was superior to Abraham's and that she was considered his "crown." Further, Abraham listened*

childless, Sarai gives her Egyptian maidservant, Hagar, to Abram as a concubine, hoping she can claim a child through Hagar.

But when Hagar becomes pregnant, Sarai feels that Hagar looks down on her because Sarai cannot conceive. Sarai treats her harshly, and Hagar flees to the desert. There an angel of God tells Hagar to return to Sarai and serve her mistress. The angel also tells her that God will increase her offspring. They will be great in number. And because God has noticed Hagar's suffering, she will bear a son, who will be named Ishmael.

After Hagar returns, God once again appears to Abram and says, "Walk in My ways and be blameless, and I will establish a covenant between Me and you and make you the father of nations. You shall no longer be called Abram. Your name will be Abraham (Avraham), the father of many nations."

God says to Abraham, "As for Sarai, your wife, do not call her Sarai, but Sarah (Sara). I will bless her, and she will give rise to nations. Rulers will come from her."

On hearing this Abraham falls down and laughs, thinking, *Shall a baby be born to a one-hundred-year-old man? And shall Sarah, at ninety years old, give birth?* God tells Abraham to name his future son Isaac, with whom the everlasting covenant will continue.

Sometime later, while Abraham is sitting at the entrance of their tent in the hot part of the day, he looks up to see three men (some commentaries call them angels) standing near him. He runs toward them, bows to the ground,

WHY ARE SARAI'S (SARAH'S) AND ABRAM'S (ABRAHAM'S) NAMES CHANGED?

to and obeyed her words because he recognized her superiority.

God makes a covenant—first with Abram and then with Sarai—about giving rise to a new nation. Their names change when it's time to signify their new roles. Naming is important in the Bible—sometimes names are given by a husband, sometimes by a wife, but the most important names are the ones given directly by God. "In fact, much of the drama in Genesis revolves around the giving of names" (Frankel, Five Books, p. 20).

God hears the cry of the boy, and an angel calls to Hagar, saying, "Do not be afraid, for God has heard your child's crying."

God opens Hagar's eyes, and she sees a well. She gives Ishmael water to drink. God is with the boy, and he grows up and becomes an archer, living in the wilderness of Paran, and his mother finds him a wife from Egypt.

Then God tests Abraham and tells him to take Isaac to the land of Moriah, where he is to offer Isaac as a burnt offering on a mountain that God will show him.

Abraham, Isaac, two servants, and a donkey travel to the place that God spoke of. The donkey carries wood that Abraham split, as well as a flint, or firestone, and a knife. As they get closer to the mountain, Abraham tells the servants to stay with the donkey and wait for Isaac and him to return. Abraham loads the wood for the offering onto Isaac's back and takes the firestone and the knife. The two of them, father and son, walk together. Then Isaac asks, "Father, I see the firestone and wood, but where is the lamb for the offering?"

"God will provide it," Abraham answers him.

When Abraham and Isaac come to the place God shows them, Abraham

How Do Other Religions Respond to the Binding of Isaac?

In the Muslim tradition, one of the rituals during hajj—the great yearly pilgrimage to Mecca—is the stoning of Satan. Pilgrims do this because in their telling of the story of Abraham's would-be sacrifice of Isaac, Satan tries to persuade Abraham against doing any such thing, thus disobeying God's specific command. There is also a similar midrash in Judaism. In fact, the story of the Binding of Isaac is one of the most contentious and difficult stories in the Bible. And much of modern commentary doesn't break down between religions, but along a gender divide—women often say that Abraham should have offered himself up as they believe Sarah would have surely done.

What Is Sarah's Reaction to Abraham's Offering?

There is nothing in the biblical text that speaks of Sarah's reaction or that tells us if she knew about the plan ahead of time. Some rabbis teach that the stories of the binding of Isaac and Sarah's death follow one another to indicate that Sarah

builds an altar and arranges the wood. Then he binds Isaac and puts him on top of the altar.

Just as Abraham reaches for his knife, an angel of God calls to him, saying, "Abraham! Abraham!"

"Here I am," he answers.

"Do not stretch out your hand against Isaac," the angel says. "For I know that you are a God-fearing man since you have not withheld your son from Me."

Abraham looks up and sees a ram caught in the thicket by its horns. It is the ram that Abraham offers in place of Isaac.

The angel of God calls a second time from Heaven and says, "I will bless you and make your offspring as numerous as the stars of heaven and the grains of sand on the seashore."

Abraham and his servants return to Beersheba. (There isn't mention of where Isaac goes.)

Sarah dies at age 127 in Kiriat Arba in the land of Canaan, now Hebron, a city nineteen miles south of Jerusalem in the Judean Hills. Abraham stays by her side, mourning and weeping for her. She is buried in the Cave of Machpelah, which Abraham buys for four hundred shekels of silver from Ephron the Hittite.

died as a result of Abraham's near sacrifice of Isaac. The Midrash Leviticus Rabba (one of the oldest midrashic works, thought to be from the fifth century CE) relates that Sarah was told by the devil that Abraham had almost killed Isaac, and she at once cried out in grief and died (My Jewish Learning).

It is also said that the near-sacrifice of Isaac was a lesson that there should be no more human sacrifice, something that was common at that time in history. There are also midrashim about Sarah taking Isaac's place as the sacrifice. The Binding of Isaac, as this section of the Bible is known, is difficult for many readers to grapple with, and much commentary has been written about it in different traditions.

IS THERE ANYTHING UNUSUAL ABOUT SARAH'S BURIAL?

The Cave of Machpelah and the nearby field were purchased by Abraham at a huge price. There is much scholarly commentary about how that field was the first tillable land purchased by a Jew in the Promised Land, which makes Sarah's burial site very memorable. The burial site in Hebron is now sacred to Jews, Christians, and Muslims.

Imagine Sarah

My sister, I am old. I have seen much and regret some. When you are young, well, some things seem important.

Abraham was a good husband to me. He was kind and he loved me. He treated me like a princess. I was a princess who served others and was happy to do that alongside my husband.

Of the two of us, I was the one who wanted a child. I wanted one so much that when I couldn't conceive, I gave Abraham my maidservant, Hagar. I thought that if she bore him a son, the boy would be like my own. But after Hagar gave birth, she treated me as if I were the servant. And her son was a wild boy. I had no influence over him.

When I bore Isaac in my old age, my relationship with Hagar grew worse. She became even more guarded, suspicious. She hissed like a serpent in my face when Abraham was not there to see.

One day I saw Ishmael "playing" with his bow and arrows near my Isaac, shooting the arrows near my boy. That day I ran to Abraham.

"You must send her and her son into the desert," I called out. "One of them is going to hurt Isaac. Tomorrow or the next day. Soon." And I told him of what I had seen.

Abraham tried to calm me. "Sit," he said. "Breathe. I don't think Ishmael will hurt his brother. He is rough, yes. But not so mean as that."

Yet I had seen Hagar's meanness. Seen her laughing as Ishmael shot his arrows.

"I am not as sure of this as you," I said more calmly. "Remember, now. God told you, 'Listen to Sarah.' Please, Abraham, listen to me. I am afraid. Hagar and I cannot live together in this place. It has become unbearable."

Abraham sat quietly. He is a man who welcomes people to his tent. He gives people food and water and washes their feet. He makes their journey easier as they travel through these desert lands. It is not like him to send someone out into the wilderness. And certainly not his own son.

But he did this for me, his princess. With his lips firmly set, he watched Hagar and Ishmael walk away from our camp, carrying sacks of food and water. Hagar was angry and crying. Ishmael was confused, yelling, "Father!" and pulling on Hagar to return.

I stood silently near Abraham, hoping that my fears would go with them.

Sarah Laughed

Sarah was a beauty,
a beauty and a half,
though nowhere does it say
that she knew how to laugh.

Until the day that Sarah—
who was nearly ninety-one—
was told by an angel
that she would bear a son.

And then she laughed.

Sarah was a beauty
on the day that she gave birth.
A son to cradle in her arms,
and populate the earth.

The mother of a son,
grandmother to a nation,
raising Isaac to a man
was quite an obligation.

That's when she stopped laughing.

3

Rebecca

Mother of Nations

Rebecca's long trek *to motherhood and the birth of her contentious twins, Jacob and Esau, who each becomes the head of a nation, begins with courage and moves through trickery. She uses both in order to follow God's directive: that her eldest son should serve his younger brother. She is a woman of greatness and a mother of two nations.*

Rebecca, the second of the four matriarchs, appears in the Bible in the Book of Genesis, chapters and verses 24:1–67, 25:19–28, 26:6–11, and 27:5–28:5.

Rebecca's (Rivka's) story begins when Abraham, well on in years and blessed by God in all things, calls the servant who is in charge of Abraham's household. Abraham is sending him on a special mission. "Do not take a wife for my son from the Canaanites. Go to my land and my relations and take a wife for Isaac."

So the servant takes ten of Abraham's camels, many gifts, and some men, and goes to Aram Naharaim, to the city of Nahor.

In time, they reach the well outside the city. It is evening, the time when the women come to draw water.

The servant says, "God of my master, Abraham, show kindness. May it happen that when I say to one of the women, 'Please let your pitcher down so I may drink,' she will answer, 'Drink and I will give your camels water also.' And so by her answer, I will know she is the one for Isaac."

Even before he finishes speaking, Rebecca, daughter of Bethuel, who was the son of Abraham's brother, Nahor, comes to the well with a pitcher on her shoulder. She is fair to look at and unmarried.

The servant runs toward Rebecca. "Please let me drink a little from your pitcher."

"Drink, my lord," she says. "And I will also draw water for your camels."

After he drinks, Rebecca runs back and forth to the well for water for all his camels.

The servant watches her, amazed. When the camels finish drinking, he gives Rebecca a golden nose ring and two gold bracelets for her arms. "Whose daughter are you?" he asks. "Is there room in your father's house for us to stay the night?"

> ### ALL THIS MARRYING OF COUSINS—WAS IT UNUSUAL?
>
> *Isaac and Rebecca are cousins through their fathers. In those days, within tribes or religious-based communities, marrying a cousin was the normal way to make certain one kept children and property within the tribe or family. It also helped ensure that a spouse worshipped the proper God. Remember that the Egyptian pharaohs married their own sisters at one point in history.*

"I am the daughter of Bethuel, who is the son of Milcah and Nahor. Yes, there is straw and feed for the animals at home, and also room for you to spend the night."

Rebecca runs and tells her family about their guests. Her brother, Laban, sees the golden nose ring and the bracelets on his sister's arms. He goes to Abraham's servant to lead him and his camels to the house.

"I am a servant of Abraham's, whom God has blessed with sheep and cattle, silver and gold, servants, camels and donkeys," the servant tells Laban. "Sarah, my master's wife, bore Abraham a son, Isaac, when Abraham was old. My master bade me travel to his father's house and find a wife for his son."

And the servant tells of Abraham's words, and his own prayers, and of meeting Rebecca at the well. "And now if you will deal kindly and truthfully with my master, tell me, and if not, tell me, that I may know."

Then Laban and his father, Bethuel, say, "The matter comes from God. Here, take Rebecca and go, and let her be a wife to your master's son."

At these words, the servant thanks God and gives objects of gold and silver and fine garments to Rebecca and gifts to her brother and mother. He and his men eat and drink, and they spend the night.

The next day, Rebecca's mother and brother say, "Let the maiden remain with us for some ten days. Then you may go."

"Delay me not, now that God has made my journey successful," says Abraham's servant.

WHAT MAKES REBECCA SPECIAL?

By marrying Isaac and bearing his children, she will become "the child of destiny, the agent of this promise" (Frymer-Kensky, p. 6). Which promise? God's promise that Abraham will father a nation. This also means that Rebecca (along with Sarah before her) will mother a nation.

"We will call the maiden and ask her," they answer.

They call Rebecca and say, "Will you go with this man?"

And she says, "I will go."

Her family blesses Rebecca and sends her away.

Rebecca and her maidservants ride upon camels, following Abraham's servant.

Now Isaac, who lives in the Negev region, goes out to the field toward evening to pray. He looks up and, behold! He sees that camels are coming.

And Rebecca raises her eyes and sees Isaac. She asks the servant, "Who is that man in the field who is walking toward us?"

"He is my master, Isaac," the servant says.

Rebecca covers herself with her veil. And the servant tells Isaac everything that has happened.

Isaac brings Rebecca into what had been Sarah's tent before she died. He takes her as his wife and loves her and, in this way, is comforted after his mother's death.

Like her late mother-in-law, Sarah, before her, Rebecca isn't able to conceive a child. Isaac prays to God on her behalf, and Rebecca at last becomes pregnant. But during her pregnancy, Rebecca feels so much turmoil within her that she prays to God, asking what is going on inside her.

God speaks to her. "There are two nations in your womb.... And one people shall be stronger than the other.... And the elder shall serve the younger."

Was It Usual for a Girl to Give Permission for Marriage?

In Mesopotamia at that time, if a marriage was arranged by a brother, the woman had to give full consent or the marriage was not considered valid. In midrash it says that when Rebecca's mother and brother tell the servant, "We will call the maiden and ask her," it indicates that a woman cannot be given in marriage without her consent. She must be asked and must state her wishes (Simon and Bial, p. 48; Plaut, p. 165).

Why Do Rebecca's Twins Struggle in the Womb?

According to tradition, Rebecca was

Rebecca gives birth to twin boys, the "two nations" that God has told her about. The firstborn has a reddish complexion and is covered with hair, and Rebecca and Isaac call him Esau (Asav). The second comes out holding on to his brother's heel, and they call him Jacob (Yaacov).

As the boys grow, Esau becomes a capable hunter who loves the outdoors, while Jacob prefers a quieter life at home. Their parents each have a favorite. Isaac loves Esau, who provides him with fresh meat for stew. Rebecca favors Jacob, the quiet one who stays nearby.

One day when Jacob is cooking lentils, Esau comes inside. He says to Jacob, "Give me some of that. I am famished."

Jacob answers, "First sell me your birthright."

Esau says, "I am so hungry. Of what use is my birthright to me?"

So Esau agrees and thus rejects his birthright.

Later, when Isaac is old and his eyesight diminished, he calls Esau to him and asks that he hunt game and make a stew. Isaac says he will then bless Esau.

Rebecca overhears what Isaac says. So while Esau is away hunting, Rebecca tells Jacob what she heard. "Bring me two baby goats," she says. "I will make them into delicious food for your father, the kind he loves. You will bring the food to your father so he will eat it and bless you before he dies."

Jacob objects. "Esau is hairy, and I am not. If father feels my skin, he will know I am deceiving him. Instead of a blessing, I will receive a curse."

childless for twenty-two years until her husband petitioned God. The twins struggling in her womb becomes an omen for how they would struggle in life.

Is There a Reason Why So Many Biblical Women Have Trouble Conceiving?

Three of the four matriarchs—Sarah, Rebecca, and Rachel—have trouble conceiving. Only Leah does not. Commentators say their experiences show that the existence of the People of Israel was a miracle and that each new generation was a gift from God to a mother who would not have been able to have children naturally without God's help (Scherman, p. 124).

"Your curse will be on me, then, not you," answers Rebecca. "Listen to me." So Jacob does as his mother asks.

Then Rebecca takes some of Esau's clothes and puts them on Jacob. She covers the smooth skin of his arms and neck with goat skins and gives Jacob the food and bread to take to his father.

Jacob goes before his father. When Isaac asks, "Which of my sons are you?" Jacob says, "It is I, Esau, your firstborn."

"How is it that you found the game so quickly?" Isaac asks.

"Because God, Your God, sped my way," Jacob answers.

"Come close to me," Isaac asks, "so I may feel you, whether you are Esau or not."

Jacob moves closer. His father touches him and says, "The voice is the voice of Jacob, but the hands are the hands of Esau." Jacob's clothes also smell of Esau.

Then Isaac eats the food Jacob offers to him, and Isaac blesses Jacob with the blessing he meant for Esau. Isaac says,

> "May God give you the dew of the
>   heavens
> And of the fat places of the earth,
> And plenty of grain and wine,
> May people serve you . . .
> And you be Lord over your
>   kinsmen."

Very soon after Jacob leaves the room, Esau comes back from hunting and also brings food for his father.

Isaac asks, "Who are you?"

ISN'T REBECCA'S USE OF JACOB TO TRICK ISAAC AN IMMORAL ACT?

Perhaps. But there are a number of clever tricks in the Bible. Two examples are when Abraham tells the pharaoh that Sarah is his sister and when Esther uses her cleverness to trap the wicked Haman. Rather than feeling immoral, this type of cleverness serves to move the story in a direction favored by God. But it also serves a secondary purpose: to show people as they really are— imperfect and evolving.

WHAT IS THE DIFFERENCE BETWEEN A BLESSING AND A BIRTHRIGHT?

The brothers probably kept their

Meet Me at the Well

"I am Esau, your firstborn," is his answer.

Isaac becomes very upset and trembles with emotion. "Who came and brought me game then? And I have eaten it and blessed him. And he shall be blessed."

On hearing his father's words, Esau lets out bitter sobs and says, "Don't you have any blessing to give me?"

Isaac answers, "I have made him master over you."

But Isaac does bless Esau, saying, "By your sword you shall live, and you shall serve your brother."

Esau's hatred of his brother grows stronger because of the blessing Isaac gave him after Jacob's trick. Esau decides to kill Jacob as soon as their father dies.

Rebecca learns his plan and sends for Jacob, telling him, "You must flee to Haran, to my brother, Laban, where you will stay until your brother's anger subsides, and he forgets what you have done to him."

But to Isaac, Rebecca gives a different reason for sending Jacob away. She says she wants Jacob to find a wife from the daughters of Laban, her brother, instead of from the Hittite women.

And Isaac listens to Rebecca and sends Jacob on his way, thus unknowingly separating the two brothers so both might live.

exchange about the birthright to themselves, which only added to Esau's bitterness toward his brother. So when Jacob disguised himself as Esau and received the blessing meant for Esau, it inflamed Esau's anger. A birthright is about who inherits what. The firstborn gets more property and other types of inheritance. But the blessing is about much more. It is about the future, and about what the parent hopes the children's lives will be like. Blessings are about spiritual guidance and predictions. A person can sell a birthright since it's basically about money. But one can't sell a blessing. In Jacob and Esau's case, the blessing was given to the wrong person and by trickery.

Imagine Rebecca

You might wonder how I feel now, with my beloved son Jacob so far away, living with my brother, Laban, and his family. I have not seen Jacob for twenty years. Yet I can still hear God's voice in my ear.

"There are two nations in your womb . . .
And the elder shall serve the younger."

It is these words that have kept me whole all this time. These words have guided me and given me strength to do what I needed to do.

It isn't that I don't love both my sons. I love Esau, too, he who came out of me red and hairy and bawling. I was glad to see Isaac shine his love on Esau, appreciating his hunting skills and his careful preparation of food. But I knew all the while that I needed to be watchful of the prophecy and guard it.

It is I who grew up in a household where trickery ruled, with a brother who was greedy and deceitful. I disdained such behavior and always strived to commit myself to honest dealings in this world. Yet I am the one who convinced Jacob to deceive his father. And then I deceived Isaac further about the real reason I wanted Jacob sent to Laban. It was not so much so that Jacob could find a wife from among Laban's daughters, but to separate my twin sons and prevent bloodshed between them. I sent one away to save them both.

Why did I not tell my husband, Isaac, about the words God said to me? Deep inside I knew that God spoke to only me for a reason and gave me this knowledge so I would be careful to guard it. And this I did.

All my life, I have not been one to doubt. Did I hesitate when Abraham's servant—I learned later that his name was Eliezer—asked for water for himself and his camels? No. I drew them water. Did I doubt when this stranger, Eliezer, asked if I would go with him and become Isaac's wife? No. I said, "I will go." God told me the elder would serve the younger. And as I watched my two boys grow, I saw the older one become a cunning man of the field, while the younger is a quiet man who lives more in the world of the spirit. In this, I saw the wisdom of God's words. The quieter way can be a measure of true strength. And I did not doubt. When the moment came, I acted to ensure that Jacob would rule over his brother.

Rebecca the Matriarch

Young woman at the well
of life,
the asked and asked-for special
wife,
the mother who at birth's
creation
helped to bear the Hebrew
nation.
Two babies quarreled there in your
womb.

You had to give them separate
room.
As God had told you—youngest
first,
a warning you once thought the
worst.
But cleverness made this come
true.
You did what God would have you
do.

4

Rachel and Leah

Sister Wives

Two sisters: *One beautiful, desirable, loved, and barren. One plain, shy, unloved, and able to bear children. Throw in some trickery, a bit of heartbreak, and here is the story of the beginning of the twelve tribes of Israel. The sisters Rachel and Leah are at the center of the story, and their struggle is their children's struggle. This story reads almost like a fairy tale.*

Rachel and Leah, the third and fourth
of the four matriarchs, appear in the
Bible in the Book of Genesis,
chapters and verses
29:1–31:44, 32:22,
33:1–2, 35:16–20,
and 49:29–33.

*L*eaving his family after tricking his brother, Esau, out of Isaac's blessing, Jacob journeys far from home until he comes to the Syrian-Arabian desert.

Ahead of him, Jacob sees a well with flocks of sheep around it. A large stone covers the mouth of the well.

"My friends, where are you from?" he asks the shepherds.

"From Haran," they answer.

"Do you know Laban, the son of Nahor? He is my uncle, my mother's brother."

"We do," they answer, pointing. "And there is his daughter Rachel coming with the flock. We wait until all the flocks are present. Then together we roll that heavy stone from the well's mouth and water our sheep."

Jacob looks at the beautiful Rachel. Filled with joy at seeing this daughter of his mother's brother, he runs to the well. With all his strength, he rolls the stone to the side and waters his uncle's flock. Then he kisses his cousin and weeps.

"I am your cousin, your father's sister's son," Jacob tells her.

Excited by this news, Rachel runs home to let her father know about her cousin whom she met at the well.

When Rachel's father, Laban, hears her news, he hurries to the well himself. There he embraces Jacob, and says, "Surely you are my bone and my flesh. Come to my house and tell me about my sister, Rebecca."

AGAIN, A YOUNG WOMAN AT THE WELL?

Rachel's arrival at the well just as Jacob reaches Haran is an auspicious omen. To meet young maidens on first entering a city is a sure sign that fortune is favorable to one's undertakings. This was true of the servant who met Rebecca when looking for a wife for Isaac; of Jacob, who met Rachel; and Moses, who met Zipporah—all at wells (Scherman, p. 147). In desert countries from biblical times until the early twentieth century, much of a tribe's daily gatherings happened at wells. It was the only place that water for daily routines—watering animals, cooking meals, washing, drinking—could regularly be found.

IS RACHEL REALLY MORE BEAUTIFUL THAN LEAH?

The Bible hardly describes either of them. Leah's beauty, or lack of it, is

And so Jacob stays with Laban and serves him for a month.

Laban says to him, "Just because you are my relative, should you serve me for nothing? Tell me, what shall your wages be?"

Jacob is thoughtful before speaking. From his first sight of her at the well, Jacob has fallen in love with Rachel. Leah, her older sister, is plain in comparison.

"I will work for you for seven years for your younger daughter, Rachel," Jacob says, "so she will be my wife."

"Better I give her to you than to an outsider," Laban says to Jacob. "Remain with me."

So Jacob works for Laban for seven years. The years seem like only a few days because of Jacob's love for Rachel.

When the seven years are over, Laban gathers the people and prepares a feast. In the evening, Laban brings the heavily veiled bride to Jacob's tent. Laban also gives her his servant Zilpah as a maid.

It isn't until the morning light that Jacob realizes he has been deceived. He has married Leah instead of his beloved Rachel.

"What is this you have done to me?" Jacob accuses Laban. "I worked for seven years so I could have Rachel as my wife. Why did you deceive me?"

"It's not the custom here to marry off the younger before the older," says Laban. "Let's complete our week of celebration for Leah. Then I will give you

often taken from the description of her eyes as "heavy" or "weak," though the medieval commentator Rashi wrote that she has "tender" eyes because she is sad. Dr. Gabriel Cohen explains that the Targum Onkelos states that Leah has "beautiful eyes." Perhaps Leah only seems dull when compared with Rachel. Or perhaps Jacob's overwhelming adoration of Rachel makes her seem more beautiful than she really is.

WHY IS HAVING SO MANY BABIES IMPORTANT IN THE BIBLE?

Having many children in order to increase the family and tribe was essential in biblical days. This was especially important because babies (and mothers) often died in childbirth, and many children never made it beyond toddler age because medicine was not very advanced.

Rachel, too, if you promise to work for me for seven more years."

Jacob agrees, and after the week of celebration is over, Laban gives him Rachel as his wife. Laban also gives Rachel a maidservant named Bilhah.

Jacob loves Rachel more than Leah, and he works for Laban for another seven years.

God sees that Leah is unloved and opens her womb. Leah has four sons: Reuben, Simeon, Levi, and Judah. After each birth she thinks she will gain Jacob's love. Rachel cannot conceive a child and is jealous of her sister.

So Rachel gives her maid, Bilhah, to Jacob. In this way, Bilhah may have a son in Rachel's place. Bilhah has two sons, Dan and Naftali.

Since Leah has not born a child in a while, she gives her maid, Zilpah, to Jacob as a concubine, and Zilpah bears two sons, Gad and Asher.

Then Leah's womb fills again, and she has a fifth son, Issachar, a sixth, Zebulun, and a daughter, Dinah.

Finally God answers Rachel's prayers and opens her womb. She has a son, Joseph.

During the years Jacob works for Laban, he grows prosperous and comes

HOW IS JACOB FOOLED, AND HOW DOES HE REACT?

"When [Leah] was led into the nuptial chamber, the guests extinguished all the candles, much to Jacob's amazement. But their explanation satisfied him. 'Thinkest thou,' they said, 'we have as little sense of decency as thy countrymen?' Jacob therefore did not discover the deception practiced upon him until morning.

"During the night Leah responded whenever he called for Rachel, and he reproached her bitterly when daylight came. 'O thou deceiver, daughter of a deceiver, why didst thou answer me when I called Rachel's name?'

"'Is there a teacher without a pupil?' asked Leah in return. 'I but profited by thy instruction. When thy father called thee Esau, didst thou not say, 'Here am I?'" (Ginzberg, "Abraham").

There is also midrash about Rachel and Jacob devising certain code words in case Laban had plans to trick Jacob. But because of Rachel's compassion for her sister, she tells Leah the code words so Leah will not be shamed. As a result, Jacob is deceived just as his father, Isaac, had been fooled.

HOW MANY CHILDREN DOES JACOB FATHER, AND WHY ARE THEY IMPORTANT?

All together the mothers of Jacob's offspring (Rachel, Leah, and the maidservants Bilhah and Zilpah)

meet me at the well

had thirteen children—twelve boys and one girl. Tradition has it that the sons "fathered" the famous twelve tribes of the Jewish people. That began the process of changing the people of the One God from a family into the promised nation. Rachel and Leah—sisters, enemies, friends—were the very center of that change (Scherman, p. 149).

WHERE EXACTLY ARE RACHEL'S AND LEAH'S TOMBS?

The traditional place of Rachel's tomb is in Bethlehem. The tomb has long been a pilgrimage site. Women who can't conceive come to pray for a child, asking Rachel to intercede with God on their behalf. "There is a custom of measuring the tomb with red woolen threads, which are then tied to children and the sick to bring good health, healing" (Skolnick, p. 48). The threads are also tied around a woman's belly to ensure a safe pregnancy.

Leah's tomb's name, Machpelah, is understood to mean "double," interpreted as a double cave, or the place where couples are buried. It is situated near Hebron. This is the same tomb where Sarah, Abraham, Rebecca, and Isaac are buried. It is also said that Adam and Eve are buried there. Today there is a wall around the area, attributed to the time of Herod the Great (Skolnick, pp. 325–327).

to own large flocks of sheep, goats and donkeys, maids, and manservants. Jacob is aware that Laban's sons are saying bad things about him. They feel that he has stolen Laban's wealth. They don't care that Laban changes Jacob's wages more than once and cheats Jacob in other ways.

Finally God says to Jacob, "Return to your homeland, where you were born, and I will be with you."

Jacob tells Rachel and Leah how Laban has been treating him and that God has told him to leave this land. Rachel and Leah agree he should do as God has told him to do.

Jacob places his children and wives on camels and drives off with them and all his livestock to go to Canaan, where his father, Isaac, still lives.

On the journey to Canaan, Rachel bears a second son, Benjamin. She dies in childbirth and is buried along the way in what is now Bethlehem. Jacob builds a tomb to mark her grave.

Jacob and Leah and the rest of the caravan reach Hebron in Canaan and reunite with Isaac. Leah, too, dies before Jacob. She is buried in the Cave of Machpelah with Abraham and Sarah and Isaac and Rebecca. After Jacob dies, he is buried there also.

Imagine Rachel

Love at first sight. That's what happened to me when I saw a stranger standing by the well seven years ago. There was something familiar about him, yet he wasn't at all like the other young men I knew. And the way he looked at me, fixing me with that gaze. I could see strength and certainty and surprise in his eyes. Then he moved that big rock alone without any help, though none of the shepherds had ever been able to do such a thing. I knew him as one favored by God. He came to me to introduce himself.

"I am Rebecca's son, your father's sister's son."

His kinsman's kiss made me shiver pleasantly, and I ran to tell my father, Laban, about this man. But really I ran to keep myself from kissing him back.

Now on the night I should be able to finally kiss him back, my father has made me sit here in my tent with guards around me so I will obey his terrible order.

I shudder with the horror of it. I know my father is not always to be trusted to stand by his word, but I did not expect this. Now he tells me, "The older must marry first, then the younger. It's our custom." I want to spit on the ground a thousand times.

It isn't my sister's fault. She has no choice in this either. But this will change everything between us. Knowing she is with Jacob and I am not—I cannot bear it.

Rachel Speaks

Sister, how hard it is to be the younger,
always last to the wedding feast.
Though now I am weighted with gold,
the only coin I wanted then was a child.
I was not, you were not, always kind.
We all, at last, grow old.
And by the end can bind.

Imagine Leah

I keep looking back through the veils at my sister's tent. My father must have bound her hands and feet together to keep her there. Me he has to push and push.

"I do not want to do this, Father," I whimper. "You promised Rachel to Jacob, not me."

My father pushes me forward again. "I know what I am doing, daughter," he says. "This will be best for the family. You will see."

I am not stupid. I do not see the good in this for me or Rachel or the family. What will Jacob say when he realizes he has married me and not his beloved Rachel? He will be angry with me, thinking I wanted this deception. Will I tell him the truth? Will he even believe me if I do?

I feel my father next to me. He's smiling. He's probably pleased with his scheme to keep Jacob with him, raising his new father-in-law's sheep and goats. He will probably trick Jacob into working many more years for Rachel. I can no longer see my sister's tent, for it is behind me. I dare not look back. I must have only Jacob before me.

I am wearing her scent, her clothes, her jewelry, but I am not Rachel. Jacob will soon discover this. My father says I am to wear the veils as long as I can. They and the darkness and the wine will fool Jacob until it is morning and too late for him to give me back.

I will be like a gift that, once given, cannot be returned.

Leah Speaks

Sister, we were tender-eyed, small-waisted,
gold in our ears, five shekels weight;
we should have been twins.
I thought the one with the most sons wins.
But love separated us; I did not mind.
I was, like Jacob, purposefully blind.
It took me to the last to bind.

5

Miriam
(and Some about Jocheved and Zipporah)

Keeping a Nation Alive

Circling around *the towering figure of Moses, who is perhaps the most famous person in the Hebrew Bible, is a group of strong women. The group includes Moses's sister, Miriam (Miryam); his mother, Jocheved (Yocheved); his wife, Zipporah (Tsiporah); the midwives; and Pharaoh's daughter. Without these women, there could be no Moses. He would have died as an infant during the great purge of Jewish boy babies. Or he might have died at the hands of Pharaoh, or when he was running from Egypt, or at the Red Sea. Or he could have died while leading the people for forty years through the desert. These women quite literally kept him alive.*

Miriam appears in the Bible in the Book of Exodus, chapters and verses 2:4–10 and 15:19–21, and in the Book of Numbers, chapters and verses 12:1–16 and 20:1–2. Jocheved appears in the Book of Exodus, chapters and verses 2:1–10 and 6:20, and in the Book of Numbers, 26:59. Zipporah appears in the Book of Exodus, chapters and verses 2:16, 2:18, 2:21–22, 4:24–26, and 18:1–6.

Anew king, or pharaoh, comes into power in Egypt and tells his people, "The Children of Israel are too many and too strong. We must deal shrewdly with them because if there is a war, they will join with the enemy and fight us."

So the Egyptians set taskmasters over the Israelites and force them into hard labor. The Israelites build cities for Pharaoh. The Egyptians make the Israelites' lives bitter with hard work both in the fields and with mortar and brick. Even so, the Israelites continue to multiply.

Then Pharaoh says to the Hebrew midwives, "When you tend to a Hebrew woman who is giving birth, if it is a boy, you will kill him. If it is a girl, you will let her live."

But the midwives fear God more than they fear Pharaoh, so they do not follow this command. They let the baby boys live and give excuses to Pharaoh. "The Hebrew women are not like the Egyptian women," they say. "Before the midwives arrive, they have already given birth."

God rewards the midwives, and the Israelites increase in number.

The angry pharaoh commands all his people, "Every son that is born to the Israelites you will throw into the river. Every daughter you will let live."

It is after this decree that Jocheved and Amram—Miriam and Aaron's

WHO WAS THE NEW PHARAOH OF EGYPT WHO BUILT THE CITIES?

Most scholars believe the pharaoh was Ramses II, who reigned from 1279 to 1213 BCE and was at one time considered a great builder of temples and other public buildings. But archeologist Werner Keller has pointed out that "when [the experts] examined the buildings a little more closely . . . [they realized that] many of these buildings must have been built centuries before . . . however Ramses II decided to have his monogram carved on them all" (Keller, p. 120). So we're not sure who the pharaoh in the Bible story is.

WHY ARE THE MIDWIVES SO IMPORTANT?

The midwives are the first people in Egypt to resist a dictate from the pharaoh, when they refuse to kill the Hebrew boy babies in "what might be history's first recorded instance of civil disobedience" (Williams, p. 26). These biblical midwives were called

mother and father—have another baby boy, Moses. Jocheved sees that the child is healthy and hides him for three months. When he grows too big to be safely hidden, she takes a wicker basket and smears it with clay and pitch to make it watertight. She places her baby inside and puts the basket among the reeds on the riverbank. His big sister, Miriam, hides a short distance away so she can watch what happens to him.

Pharaoh's daughter goes down to the river with her maidservants to bathe. Seeing the basket among the reeds, she sends her maidservant to bring the basket to her. When Pharaoh's daughter opens the basket and sees the crying baby, she takes pity on him and says, "This is one of the Hebrew boys."

Miriam bravely steps out of hiding and speaks to Pharaoh's daughter. "Shall I go and find one of the Hebrew women to nurse this baby for you?"

"Go," says Pharaoh's daughter.

Miriam brings Jocheved to Pharaoh's daughter.

"Take this boy and nurse him for me," says Pharaoh's daughter. "And I will pay you."

So Jocheved takes her own baby home and nurses him and cares for him. When the boy grows older, Jocheved brings him to Pharaoh's daughter, and he becomes her son.

Shifra and Pu'ah. Some commentaries say that Shifra was probably Jocheved, Moses's mother, while Pu'ah was really Miriam, his sister. In the Bible it says, "It was because the midwives feared God that God made houses for them." This, the rabbis explain, means that they became the start of great dynasties.

IS JOCHEVED IMPORTANT FOR MORE THAN BEING MOSES'S MOTHER?

Jocheved is the mother of three of the most famous children in the Hebrew Bible: Moses, who brought his people safely out of servitude in Egypt and who received the Ten Commandments on Mount Sinai; Aaron, the high priest and father of all Kohanim, the priests of the Jewish people; and Miriam, a prophetess who brought water to the wandering Jews in the desert, helping keep them alive for forty years. But more than just a mother, in some sources Jocheved is called the chief nurse for the Jews of Egypt.

Pharaoh's daughter decides to name him Moses, explaining, "I drew him out of the water." ("Mo" is the Egyptian word for water and "uses" is the verb "to save from water.")

And so it is that Moses grows up in Pharaoh's palace and becomes an Egyptian prince. Later he kills an Egyptian who is beating a Hebrew and escapes to the land of Midian.

In Midian, Moses meets Zipporah and her six sisters, who are all daughters of the Midianite priest Jethro. They come to a local well to water their sheep, but some shepherds drive them off. Moses rises to their defense and waters their flock. When Zipporah tells her father about the stranger who saved them, Jethro gives Zipporah to Moses as a wife.

Moses doesn't come back to Egypt for many years, until he is called upon by God to approach Pharaoh with Aaron, his brother, to demand the release of the Israelites.

Pharaoh is stubborn and it takes God sending ten plagues, including the death of Pharaoh's firstborn son, to convince him to let the Israelites go. Even then, after he releases them,

WHO WAS PHARAOH'S DAUGHTER?

Though Pharaoh's daughter is never named in the Bible, many scholars think she is Thouoris, one of the many daughters of Ramses II. Others believe that she was Merrhi or Myrrina or Mercis. Still others feel she was known as Bithiah, Bathia, or Batya. There is no consensus about which daughter it was. The great writer of antiquity Josephus called her Thermuthis. It's not surprising we don't know which of Pharaoh's daughters she is—he had fifty-nine!

Why did she pick the baby up? The Bible says simply: "She took pity on him." But rabbinical commentaries offer many other reasons, including that she was childless and wished to adopt him or that she was angry with her father and wanted to thwart his wishes. A more folktale-like reason comes from Exodus Rabbah: "Pharaoh's daughter suffered from leprosy, which is the reason she had come to the river to bathe, but as soon as she touched the basket in which tiny Moses lay, she was healed" (Klapholtz, p. 604).

In the Qur'an (the Muslim religious text), the woman who picks Moses up is Pharaoh's wife; she raises him so that someday he may be of use to Pharaoh's plans.

meet me at the well

BESIDES SAVING BABY MOSES, WHY IS MIRIAM IMPORTANT?

Supposedly, Miriam was only five years old when she prophesied that her mother would have a son who would save the Jewish people. That marked the beginning of her prophesies. By the time Moses led the Jews out of Egypt, Miriam was already known for being a leader among women, nourishing her people, and being able to prophesy the future.

WHO WAS ZIPPORAH?

Zipporah was a Midianite, a member of an Arab people who possibly lived in the desert areas of southern Transjordan, northern Arabia, and the Sinai. They were descendants of a man named Midian, who is sometimes identified as a son of Abraham by his second wife. They were probably nomadic herdsmen who worshipped many gods.

Even though Zipporah was neither Jewish nor Egyptian—both religions Moses knows well—she and Moses were married and had two sons, Gershom and Eliezer. Moses lived happily with his Midianite in-laws for many years until God spoke to him from a burning bush, saying, "The cry of the Israelites has reached me. I will send you to Pharaoh, and you shall free the Israelites from Egypt." So Moses and Zipporah and their sons left Midian for Egypt.

Pharaoh changes his mind and sends his army—chariots and all—in pursuit.

When Moses holds out his arm, God brings a strong east wind over the Red Sea. The Red Sea parts, the Israelites cross on dry land to the other side, and the pursuing Egyptians drown in the returning waters.

On the other side of the Red Sea, the Israelites sing a song of victory and the prophetess Miriam (who reappears for the first time since her brother Moses was taken to Pharaoh's palace as an infant) takes up a tambourine. All the women follow her with their own tambourines, dancing, while Miriam chants, "Sing to God, Who has triumphed, having hurled horse and rider into the sea."

Was It Really the Red Sea, and Did the Waters Really Part?

Many Bible scholars and archaeologists feel that the Red Sea may not be the place of the ancient crossing. They insist that the Hebrew words taken to mean "Red Sea" (yam suph) should instead be translated as "Sea of Reeds" which could be either the Bitter Lakes, a reedy marshland north of the Gulf of Suez, or Lake Timsah, between Port Said and Suez.

There's a phenomenon called "wind set-down effect" that occurs less than once every 2,400 years. Such a wind could have exposed an underwater ridge, and the Israelites might have crossed over the ridge without getting their feet wet. By the time the Egyptians followed, the effect could have dissipated—at least that's the theory.

But the story offers a truth beyond any actual facts—it is a tale about enslavement and escape, a story of obedience and trust, and a story that emphasizes the community of the Jewish people and how, by listening to their prophets, they were set free.

A Midrash About Miriam Supplying the Wandering Jews with Water

While wandering in the desert for forty years after leaving Egypt (as the Bible says), the Israelites were thirsty, so God created a well in honor of Miriam, and it followed wherever she went. The well was in the shape of a sieve-like rock. Whenever the Israelites camped, the well appeared nearby on a high spot opposite the entrance of the Tent of Meeting. When the leaders of the twelve tribes sang, "Spring up, O well," water shot into the air like a geyser, creating streams that provided water for all the people and their animals.

After Miriam died, the well disappeared. But it was said that if a person went up to the summit of Mount Carmel and saw a kind of sieve in the Sea of Tiberias, that was Miriam's Well. In honor of her leadership and good deeds, Miriam became mother of a royal line: Bezalel, the builder of the Holy Sanctuary, is descended from her, as is David, King of Israel.

It has become a custom in some Jewish families to place a "Cup of Miriam" filled with water next to the wine cup for Elijah during the Passover seder, the dinner that recounts the Exodus of the Israelites from their slavery in Egypt to freedom and to serve God.

Imagine Miriam

I am so happy at this moment. My people and I have finally left Egypt behind and see freedom ahead. The Egyptians who enslaved us, forced us into hard labor, made our lives intolerable, and ordered that our boy babies be killed are gone. Drowned in the sea. We stand on this shore, shocked, relieved, amazed, joyful, and, yes, a little afraid of what lies before us.

I grab my tambourine from the sack on my back. Of course, I have my tambourine. The men laughed at us when we packed them with our wheat and bowls and tents. But we women took them for just such a moment like this.

I tap the tambourine louder and louder in rhythm to my song. "Sing to God," I cry, "Who has triumphed so gloriously."

I dance, leading the other women, who also grab their tambourines. Soon we are a circle of dancing women, girls, toddlers. Laughing, jumping, screaming our joy. For what a day this is!

I know there will be rough times ahead, but we are on our journey now—to a new land with my brothers, Moses and Aaron, leading the way. And me, too.

Journeys always have rough spots. The important thing is we have left Egypt and enslavement, left the cruel task masters, left the cruel decrees of Pharaoh behind.

We will have to figure out what this freedom is and what it means.

For now we dance. Making time to celebrate is important, too. We begin our journey in joy.

Hiding Moses:
Six Women

In the reeds, a girl helps hide
a basket with a babe inside
from the men with sharpened knives
sent to cut short Hebrew lives.

And two midwives,
Pharaoh's daughter,
save him from
both knife and water.

His true mother waits nearby
when for a nurse, there is a cry.
Raises him to be a prince,
no one like him then—or since.

Later, well met, his new bride
is the one who now must hide
her husband in her tribe's embrace
so he can save the Hebrew race.

Oh, the courage of these six
when Moses is in such a fix.
Praise them named, and nameless, too,
who saved us all when they were through.

6

Deborah and Jael
Judge and Judgment

The first woman charismatic leader (often rendered as "judge") in Israel, the war leader and prophetess Deborah (Devorah), always spoke with a deep conscience. Before she appears in the Bible, other strong women respond to the men in their lives, men they can live comfortably with and with whom they can conceive children for the Abrahamic line. But in Deborah we find a public figure. Jael is her opposite. All we know about Jael (Yael) from the Bible is that she is the wife of Heber the Kenite. But she is also a woman who—within strict, conservative tribal protocols—still manages to do what is both extremely dangerous and absolutely necessary.

Deborah appears in the Book of Judges, which is in the Prophets section of the Bible, chapters and verses 4:1–24 and 5:3–31. Jael appears in the Book of Judges, chapters and verses 4:17–22 and 5:24–27.

$w$ell after the Israelites' Exodus from Egypt and the conquest of Canaan, the promised land, the Israelites' prophet, Ehud, dies. The Israelites lose their way and do what is offensive to God. God hands them over to King Jabin of Canaan, who oppresses Israel for twenty years.

At this time, Deborah is a prophetess and judge of Israel. It is her habit to sit under a tree named for her, the Palm of Deborah, which is located between Ramah and Bethel, in the hill country of Ephraim. The Israelites come to her for judgment.

Deborah summons Barak, son of Avinoam, and says to him, "God has commanded, 'Go and march up to Mount Tabor. Take ten thousand men of the tribes of Naftali and Zebulun with you. I, God, will draw Jabin's commander, Sisera, his chariots and troops toward you, and I will deliver him into your hands.'"

Barak answers Deborah, "If you go with me, I will go. If not, I will not go."

"I will go with you," says Deborah, "but I warn you that the path you are taking will not lead to your glory, because God will deliver Sisera into the hands of a woman."

Deborah accompanies Barak, who with her support is able to gather ten thousand men to fight Sisera's army.

When Sisera learns that Barak has gone to Mount Tabor with a fighting force, he calls for all his iron chariots and all his people.

What Does God Do About the Offenses the Israelites Committed?

According to a story based in part on a tale from Philo the Historian, when Ehud, the judge, died, there was none to take his place. And because there was no judge to interpret the laws for them, the people stopped obeying the laws. Many even stopped worshipping God.

So God sent an angel to them, saying: "Out of all the nations on earth, I chose a people for Myself, and I thought that so long as the world stands, My glory would rest upon you. I even sent Moses My servant to teach you goodness and righteousness. But as you have strayed from My ways, I will now arouse your enemies to rule over you. But should you cry out, I will send a woman unto you, and she will be a beacon to shine as a light for you for forty years" (Ginzberg, "The Judges").

That light was Deborah. She lived about three thousand years ago, the fourth judge of the "pre-monarchic"

Meet Me at the Well

Then Deborah says to Barak, "Awake! This is the day God will deliver Sisera into your hands. God is marching before you."

Barak, followed by a huge wave of confident fighting men, charges down from Mount Tabor toward Sisera and his troops.

God throws Sisera's army into a panic. Losing his own courage, Sisera leaps from his chariot and flees on foot, while Barak chases after the army. All of Sisera's men fall by the sword. Not one is left.

Meanwhile Sisera finds his way to the tent of Jael, the wife of Heber the Kenite, for there is peace between King Jabin and the family of Heber.

Jael comes out of her tent and says, "Come in, my lord. Do not fear."

So Sisera follows her into the tent, and she covers him with a blanket.

He says, "Give me some water. I'm thirsty."

She opens a skin of milk and gives it to him to drink. She covers him again so he will sleep.

Sisera says, "Stand at the entrance to the tent. If any man comes and asks if there is someone in your tent, say no!" Exhausted from running, he falls asleep.

Jael takes a tent peg and a hammer. She approaches Sisera quietly while he sleeps, then drives the peg into his temple until it pierces the ground and he dies.

Barak has been pursuing Sisera and sees Jael's tent. Jael goes out of the tent to greet him.

Israel (before there was a ruling Jewish king). Called a "Mother in Israel," Deborah may have been married to Lapidoth, whose name means "torches." Or it may have meant that she was called a "fiery woman." No one is sure.

WHAT IS THE MEANING OF DEBORAH'S TREE?

The particular palm Deborah sat under is a landmark for the Tribe of Ephraim, as well as the site where Deborah made her earlier prophecies. Some rabbis have suggested that she sat in judgment outside because it "was not becoming that men should visit a woman in her house" (Ginzberg, "The Judges").

WHY DOES BARAK ASK DEBORAH TO LEAD THE TROOPS?

Barak doesn't think he will be able to gather the troops, but he believes that the prophet Deborah—with the authority of God behind her—can rally them. In those days war leaders often waited for the local prophet to explain the signs before taking action.

"Come, I will show you the man you are looking for," she says.

Barak goes into the tent with Jael, sees Sisera lying dead with the peg in his forehead, and knows that what Deborah had foreseen has come true, for on that day God has subdued King Jabin of Canaan before the Israelites by the hand of a woman.

The Song of Deborah appears in the Bible and tells the story about Deborah, Jael, and Sisera.

On that day, Deborah and Barak, son of Avinoam, sing:

"I sing praises to God.
When You came from Seir, the earth
*   quaked, the mountains trembled.*
Until I, Deborah, arose, a mother in
*   Israel,*
Travelers went by roundabout paths
*   out of fear of marauders.*
The people lived in walled towns and
*   were not safe.*
Deliverance ceased in Israel.
When Israel chose new gods, war
*   came to its gates.*

. . .

Now chant about the gracious acts
*   of God.*
Awake, O Deborah.
Awake, awake and sing a song.

WHY DOES JAEL KILL SISERA?

There are three theories to answer this question.

First theory: Jael is the wife of a tribal chief. By their laws no man can enter her tent without asking the chief or speaking to one of the other men of the tribe. By violating the tribe's laws, Sisera gives up all rights to its protection. Even worse, by speaking to a woman without a man of her tribe present, he shames her. He also asks for water, intimating that she's a poor hostess for not offering it, thus compounding his sins utterly.

Second theory: Jael is a priestess in a religious community. Knowing this, Sisera comes specifically to ask for sanctuary. But like Deborah, Jael is directly in touch with God, who orders her to kill Sisera.

Third theory: Sisera loved Jael, and though she was married to someone else, she loved him back, so he came to be hidden by her. But when it becomes clear that he has been tracked to her tent, he asks her to kill him so she is not put in danger.

All of these theories imagine more than what appears on the pages of the Bible. They consider other passages in the Torah and also what is known about local tribal matters, cultic religions, ancient legends, and the translations of individual words. (Note: Tent "pin" and "peg" are interchangeable.)

Meet Me at the Well

IS DEBORAH'S WARNING—"BY THE HAND OF A WOMAN"—A PROPHECY?

Knowing something ahead of time and speaking about it is considered prophecy in the Bible. It is important, though, to understand that a prophecy is not meant as crystal-clear prediction of the future. Biblical prophecy is often a moral outcry to serve God, to rededicate oneself or one's tribe to God, or a specific call to action. When Deborah says, "God will deliver Sisera into the hands of a woman," she has divine foreknowledge. But Barak thinks this means that Deborah will capture Sisera, likely in battle. As rabbis and commentators throughout the ages point out, prophecies are rarely direct. It is Jael's hand, not Deborah's, that strikes the fatal blow.

WHY ARE THERE TWO SIMILAR ACCOUNTS OF DEBORAH AND JAEL?

One is a narrative; the other is a poem song. They both contain similar elements. But the Song of Deborah is thought to be much older. Look carefully—the two have slightly different agendas. Check how often Barak is mentioned in each. See how the story and poem differ in regard to how difficult the times were for the Israelites. Notice how in the story Jael kills Sisera while he sleeps, whereas in the poem it is not that clear. And only the poem mentions Sisera's mother, wondering about what she assumes will be his victory and waiting for news which comes horribly late.

Arise, O Barak,
And capture your prisoners.
Then the survivors become victorious
  over the mighty.
God's people win a victory over the
  warriors.
        .   .   .

Most blessed of women is Jael,
Wife of Heber the Kenite.
He asked for water, she gave him milk.
Her left hand reached for the tent pin
And her right for the workman's
  hammer.
She struck Sisera,
Smashed and pierced his temple.
He fell at her feet and lay there
  destroyed.
        .   .   .

Through her windows, Sisera's
  mother peered and whimpered,
'Why is his chariot so long in coming?
Why so late the clatter of his wheels?'
'They must be dividing the spoils,'
One of her ladies answers.
        .   .   .

So may Your enemies be destroyed,
  God.
And let those who love God be like
The sun rising in strength.
And the land was peaceful for forty
  years"
(Orlinsky, pp. 384–387).

Imagine Deborah

Sitting here under this sacred palm called by my name brings me a sense of wholeness and peace. I hear God's words so clearly under this tree. The people know to find me here and come with their problems: a husband and wife arguing, a child misbehaving, a goat wandering.

I am glad to be sitting again in this peaceful spot after fighting that victorious battle. Some thought me foolish for wanting to gather as many of the Israelite tribes as possible to fight the Canaanites. In the past, one tribe has always protected its own territory. But see how we, all the tribes of Israel, work together now to keep the peace in all the land?

I am "Deborah, mother of Israel." I feel that I have earned that title, though some may say I am boastful to use it in my song. If my name were Rueven or Ephraim and I called myself "Father of Israel," would they still call me arrogant? I think not. It is because I am a woman that they say these things. Never mind. I will continue to sit under this holy palm and listen to God's words, listen to the people, and speak about what I hear and see.

Yes, it is wonderful to win in battle, but even better will be the forty years of peace that God has promised us.

Song of Judgment

Deborah under the palm tree,
her face shadowed by leaves,
renders judgment for a man in pain,
for a widowed woman who grieves.

Sing your song of judgment,
O woman of the flame.
Awake. You sing of battle
and call Barak by name.

She counts the coming battles;
she prophesies the doom
of many-charioted Sisera
within a woman's room.

Sing your song of judgment,
O woman of the fire.
Mother of the Israelites,
for none is deemed the higher.

Imagine Jael

I can hear the battle. It's that close. The screams of the men and the horses. The clanging of metal on metal. Heber, my husband, thought this was a good place to set up our tents. Water nearby. Grass for grazing. Trees for shade. Now it has become a good place for fighting.

Who knows which side will win. Will it be the Israelites under Barak and Deborah? Yes, I have heard about Deborah's part in this. Such a strong woman. Everyone has heard of her prophecies and judgments in this land.

We Kenites are generally friendly with the Canaanite king, Jabin, whose forces are under the command of Sisera. But Heber and I also think of our ancestors. We remember Hobab, also called Jethro, father-in-law of Moses, who was my husband's kin. And we can't help but see the harsh treatment of Moses's people by King Jabin.

Now what is that new noise so close to our encampment? It sounds like running footsteps and cries.

I'd better stand by the tent entrance and see who it is coming this way. If the battle is upon us, I must be prepared to take sides. To defend those my heart is closest to: the Israelites. But what can one woman do? Ah, I know what Deborah would say to that.

Song of Jael

A woman's arm may rock the cradle,
stir the soup pot, bake the bread.
A woman does not raise a tent peg,
does not leave a strong man dead.

But women can be slain in battle;
women can be hurt by war.
Better raise the tent peg, sister—
know what you are fighting for.

7

Hannah
Mother of Samuel

Hannah (Chana) is a woman whose role seems simple and private: barren wife who at last becomes a mother. But what she does, that none of the other women in the Bible do, is to make a private prayer that—in today's terms—goes viral. And she also does the unthinkable by giving up a much-desired child to God because she'd promised she would. Yet in so doing, she delivers not just a child, but a man who becomes a prophet and the one to anoint the first two kings of Israel.

Hannah appears in the first Book of
Samuel, in the Prophets section of
the Bible, chapters and verses
1:1–28, 2:1–11, and
2:18–21.

$\mathcal{E}$lkanah, a man from the hill country of Ephraim, has two wives. One is Hannah and the other, Peninah. Peninah has children, but Hannah has none.

Every year Elkanah, Hannah, Peninah, and the children travel to Shiloh to worship and offer sacrifices to God. On the day of the sacrifices, Elkanah gives portions of the offerings to Peninah and all her sons and daughters. He gives only one portion to Hannah, even though she is his favorite.

Because Hannah is barren, Peninah taunts her unmercifully. She does this on purpose year after year. Elkanah doesn't understand why Hannah is so angry.

"Hannah, why are you crying? Why won't you eat?" her husband, Elkanah, asks her. "Aren't I better to you than ten children would be?"

When the family finishes eating and drinking at Shiloh, Hannah gets up. Near her, Eli the priest sits at the doorpost to the local sanctuary of God.

Hannah prays to God, crying the whole time, and makes a vow.

"Oh, God, if You will look upon my suffering and remember me, if You will grant me a son, I will dedicate him to You for his whole life."

Eli the priest watches Hannah's lips move, but because she's praying silently in her heart, he can't hear what she is saying.

So Many Men in the Bible Have More Than One Wife— Why?

It was not unusual in that place and in that time for a man to have more than one wife. We have already seen it with Abraham, who married Sarah but also had Hagar as a kind of second wife. Jacob married sisters, Leah and Rachel. Sometimes men (think of the pharaohs) had even more wives. In fact, it was more unusual for a man to have only one wife. Since giving birth was dangerous, and many babies and their mothers died in the process or soon after, a man with several wives upped the odds of having a large and thriving family. Even now, in parts of the Middle East and Africa, having multiple wives is considered ordinary.

Is It Unusual for a Woman to Pray in Biblical Times?

No—women pray all the time in the Bible. What is unusual is that

Meet Me at the Well

"How long will you act like a drunk?" Eli the priest rebukes Hannah. "You need to stay away from that wine!"

"I haven't had any wine or other strong drink, my lord," Hannah answers. "I am a very sad woman and am pouring out my heart to God."

"Go in peace then," Eli tells her. "May God grant your request."

"May your servant find favor in your eyes," Hannah answers, and goes on her way. She eats a meal and is no longer sad.

The next morning, the family wakes up, bows before God, and returns home to Ramah.

There God remembers Hannah. And it comes to pass that she conceives and bears a son. She says she names him Samuel (which can mean "God has heard" or "asked of God"), "Because I asked God for him."

The next year, when it is time for Elkanah and the whole family to return to Shiloh to offer the annual sacrifices to God, Hannah remains at home.

"I will bring the child when he stops nursing," she tells Elkanah. "Then he will stay with God."

"Do what you think is best," says Elkanah.

So Hannah stays home and cares for Samuel until he is weaned. Then, the next year, though he is still young, she takes him to the House of God in

Hannah, an ordinary woman, speaks her prayer—or psalm—from the heart. When her story was later set down in the Bible for all to read, what happened is something that didn't happen to any other woman in the Bible: her private prayer became public. It became important in the spiritual life of all Jews and set the stage for how Jews would pray from then on—a soft recitation in a quiet sanctuary. This is especially meaningful because in Hannah's time such a sanctuary would have been used mainly for animal sacrifice. As Miki Raver has written, Hannah's psalm "marks an important shift in Hebrew prayer and ritual . . . the first time a heartfelt, spontaneous prayer is recorded as the central act of Jewish worship" (Raver, p. 110).

Hannah's prayer also became an influence for the Christian Bible (see especially the Apostle Luke's version of Mary's Song in Luke 1:46–55).

Imagine Hannah

I try to avoid Peninah's tent. Besides seeing all her children playing outside, while I don't have that joy, she calls me names.

"Empty Womb," she calls me.

"My name is Hannah," I call.

I will have to find a different way back.

I dread the trip to the Temple in Shiloh tomorrow. It will not be easy to avoid Peninah's taunts then.

We have been in Shiloh now for three days and have made all the sacrifices the priests and God expect. Yet I do not feel cleansed.

In this place of sacrifices, I offer my tears and the words I pray from my heart, from the deepest places within me.

I know it's the custom to pray silently, but there is so much sadness and yearning in my heart that I find myself saying my prayers aloud, whispering them softly into the holy space. Emptying the words in my heart for God to hear.

I pray these words, "I promise You, God, that if I do conceive and bear a child, I will be so very grateful. And if the child is a boy, I will give him into Your service."

I do feel better. Something heavy has lifted in me. I look up and see the old priest Eli staring at me. He accuses me of being drunk in this holy place. But when I explain my pain, he softens.

"May God answer your prayers," he says.

"Blessings on you," I say, grateful.

My heart is full of this gratefulness. The gratefulness has pushed out all the bitterness. I want to remember this moment, this feeling. Gratefulness. Fullness. Not sadness or emptiness.

When Peninah calls me names, I will think of this moment. And I will greet my husband Elkanah, who loves me, with a full heart.

There he comes now.

Hannah's Lullaby

Sleep, my son—no angels tend thee.
Only I am near,
long years waiting for your coming.
Sleep well; I am here.

Far we trekked from home to Shiloh,
Papa, Aunt, and I.
Long I prayed to have you with me,
till God heard my cry.

Promises I made a-plenty.
One is hard to keep.
Soon you will be gone from Mama,
but, till then, pray sleep.

To God I send thee;
God will tend thee.
Sleep, my little one, sleep.

8

Naomi and Ruth

Kin and Kind

Naomi (Naomi) and her daughter-in-law Ruth (Rut), both widows, share neither a religion nor a culture. Nor are they legally bound to each other. But Ruth insists on accompanying her beloved mother-in-law back to the land of Judah to help settle Naomi on the small piece of land her late husband left her. What happens next sounds a lot like a fairy tale, and it has elements of a traditional folk narrative, but the story of Naomi and Ruth is bound up in Jewish laws and traditions such as tsedakah (charity), caring for those who are considered poor relations, marriage, religious conversion, and the treatment of immigrants (or strangers). It sets a high and conscience-driven bar for an important Jewish tradition—sympathy for others—as well as influencing the basis for both Muslim and Christian approaches to charity, especially to strangers.

The story of Naomi and Ruth is told in four chapters in the section of the Bible called *The Writings*. Megillat Ruth, the Book (or Scroll) of Ruth, was added to the Tanakh, or Jewish canon, along with four other scrolls: Song of Songs, Lamentations, Ecclesiastes, and Esther. This has led to centuries of debate as to whether these scrolls can be considered holy writ.

In the days when the judges rule, there is a famine in the land, and a man goes from Bethlehem in Judah to sojourn in Moab with his wife and their two sons.

The man, Elimelech, his wife, Naomi, and two sons, Mahlon and Chilion, leave Judah in order not to starve. But misfortune follows them to Moab, where Elimelech soon dies.

Naomi's two sons marry Moabite women, Orpah and Ruth, and they all work and live in Moab for about ten years.

Suddenly misfortune finds the family again. Mahlon and Chilion die. Their childless wives are understandably distraught, as is mother Naomi. But later Naomi hears someone say that God has once again blessed the people of Judah with good harvests. Naomi determines that she will return to Judah where she has family and a small plot of land. But what should she do about her two young, widowed daughters-in-law?

The women start to walk down the road to Judah when Naomi tells them, "Why should you go with me? Go, return home, my daughters, each to your mother's house. May the Lord deal kindly with you as you have dealt with my deceased sons and me." Then she kisses them, ready to send them on their way.

Both girls reply, "No, we will return with you to your people."

Shaking her head, Naomi reminds

WHERE IS MOAB, AND WHY IS IT IMPORTANT?

Moab lay on the eastern border of Israel and Judah, along the Dead Sea. Its population was descended from Sodom and Gomorrah, through Lot, the one man who escaped after the cities' destruction. Moab was located in what is now the modern state of Jordan. So the Jordanians and the Jews have a bond through King David, who was the great-grandson of a Moabite woman, Ruth.

Since Moabites worshipped idols, there was a lot of bad blood between them and the Jews in those days. Traditionally, Moabite women had to raise their children in their husband's religion, so the Israelites did not allow their women to marry Moab men. Moab men were not allowed to convert to Judaism, but Moabite women could convert and marry Israelite men, as Ruth did.

WHY DOES NAOMI TRY TO SEND HER DAUGHTERS-IN-LAW AWAY?

We don't know for sure. Whether Naomi is testing the young women—

them that she has no more sons to become husbands to them, nor is she likely at her age to marry and be able to provide for them. A bit lightly, she adds that even if she married that very night and could she still bear sons, "Would you wait for them until they grew up?"

Orpah understands. There is nothing binding her to Naomi anymore. So she leaves.

Ruth is of sterner stuff. Her response is considered one of the most memorable in the Bible. She tells Naomi that she will accompany her to Judah, saying, "Whither you go, I will go; wherever you lodge, I will lodge; your people shall be my people, and your God, my God. Where you die, I will die, and there I will be buried."

Naomi realizes that Ruth is truly her daughter, and she accepts that Ruth will share her fate. Off they go to the city of Bethlehem, in Judah, arriving in time for a barley harvest, and the city buzzes with excitement about their arrival.

In Judah lives a wealthy kinsman of Naomi's dead husband, Elimelech. The kinsman's name is Boaz. He owns a lot of land and has many servants. His barley fields, like those of the neighboring farmers, are open to gleaners. He is known to be especially generous.

Once they are settled, Ruth tells Naomi she will go out and glean among the ears of grain. Naomi answers, "Go, my daughter."

as some commentators believe—or worries that they will never be able to remarry in Judah since they are Moabites—is a question that has never been fully resolved. She calls them "daughters," not "daughters-in-law," to show them how close she feels to them. If she'd had other sons, the girls would have married them, for such was the custom of the time. And in true folktale fashion, she tries to send them back to Moab three times.

WHAT HAPPENS TO ORPAH AFTER THAT?

In the eighty-five verses of the Book of Ruth, Orpah is named only twice. She is defined by not going with Naomi. Ironically, by doing exactly as her mother-in-law tells her to do, Orpah ends up the outcast, the forgotten one. We don't know if she starves to death in Moab, marries again, has children, returns to the god of her childhood, or dies young. There is a folk legend about her in which she abandons herself to bad behavior and has four gigantic sons, one of whom is Goliath.

Boaz arrives at his fields and notices Ruth—whom he doesn't recognize—among the regular gleaners. He asks a servant who she is and learns that she is a Moabite woman who returned with Naomi. (In other words, the servant points out her kinship to Boaz at the same time he mentions that she is an immigrant or outsider.) He also tells Boaz that Ruth has taken care of Naomi on the road and that she is a hard worker and does not complain.

Boaz goes over to Ruth and tells her that his fields shall be open to her. He adds that if in the fields she stays close to the young women of his household, she will be under his protection and no one will bother her.

Ruth bows down in front of him and asks, "Why are you so kind as to single me out when I am a foreigner?"

Boaz tells her that he knows her history and loyalty to her mother-in-law, adding, "May you have a full reward from the Lord God of Israel, under whose wings you have come to take shelter."

At the meal break, Ruth sits next to the reapers and Boaz again shows her favor, giving her a share of the reapers' roasted grain. Afterward, when she goes off to glean some more, Boaz tells his servants, "Pretend to forget some of the grain in the bundles and leave them for her to glean, and do not reproach her when she picks them up."

Ruth works very hard that day, and she gleans about a bushel of barley to take back to Naomi. She also saves

WHY DOES RUTH REFUSE TO LEAVE NAOMI?

Presumably she stays out of deep love for her mother-in-law, who has already suffered many losses—home, husband, and both of her sons. Ruth also probably worries that Naomi will not be able to care for herself on the road, for single women her age have few options. The way Ruth tells Naomi she will stay with her is echoed in the language that Ruth's great-grandson David and his friend Jonathan use to swear allegiance to each other later in the Bible.

Though this story is called the Book of Ruth, it's really both women's stories. The writer Elie Wiesel once quipped that the scroll should have been named after Naomi, but she vetoed the idea!

some of the bread that Boaz had given her. She knows Naomi will eat well this evening.

When Ruth returns home with the barley, Naomi asks, "Where did you glean today?"

Ruth answers that the field belonged to a man named Boaz.

Then Naomi says, "Blessed be the Lord who has not failed in kindness. This man is related to us."

And so Ruth continues to work in Boaz's fields under his protection until the gleaning is done.

The evening that the gleaning is finished, Naomi tells Ruth that Boaz will be threshing the barley that very night, and he will be sleeping on the threshing floor to keep a careful watch on things.

She tells Ruth, "Go and bathe and anoint yourself and put on your best clothes and go down to the threshing floor, but do not let Boaz know you are there until after he has finished eating and drinking."

If Ruth thinks what Naomi has just told her is odd, she says nothing to show it, but listens intently.

"When he lies down," Naomi says, "you shall come and uncover his feet and lie down, and he will tell you what to do."

Ruth answers, "I will do whatever you tell me."

Once Boaz is asleep, Ruth tiptoes across the threshing floor, lifts the blanket from his feet, and lies down.

WHAT ARE GLEANERS?

Gleaners are poor people who collect leftover crops from harvested fields. In those days, it was a well-established custom for farmers to let their poorer neighbors—especially widows and orphans—pick over their fields after the harvest. This was an important part of the Jewish traditions of tsedakah, *or charity, and* gemilut hasadim, *the giving of loving-kindness.*

WHERE ARE BOAZ'S FIELDS?

Sometimes history has imaginative twists. About a mile east of Bethlehem are two fields. One is called Field of Boaz, where, by tradition, Ruth gleaned. Next to it is Shepherd's Field, where—again by tradition—the angels announced the birth of Jesus some eleven hundred years later (United Church of God).

At midnight Boaz suddenly wakens and sees Ruth, though in the dark he cannot make out who she is. He asks, "Who are you?"

She sits up. "I am Ruth, your handmaiden, and you shall spread your robe over me for you are my next of kin."

Boaz says to her, "May you be blessed of the Lord, your latest act of kindness is greater than the first, for you have not turned to younger men, whether rich or poor. Do not fear, for all the elders of my town will know that you are a worthy woman."

Then comes his warning: "It is true I am a close kinsman, but there is one even closer than I. If he redeems [lays a claim to] you, let him, but if he does not wish to redeem you, I will. Lie down again until morning."

So Ruth sleeps at his feet until dawn.

They rise very early in the morning, and Boaz says, "Let it not be known that a woman came to the threshing floor. Hold out your shawl." He shakes out six measures of barley into her shawl and puts it on her back.

And so Ruth returns in the early morning to the little house where Naomi waits, to tell her all that has happened.

Naomi nods with satisfaction, saying, "That man will not rest until he has resolved the matter today."

In fact that very morning, Boaz is already at the gate of the city where all the men gather to discuss and rule on the business and laws of the day.

WHAT IS A THRESHING FLOOR, AND WHY IS BOAZ SLEEPING THERE?

A threshing floor may be a mill building, or a place with a hard, flat surface of wood, stone, or packed earth where the stalks of grain are beaten with flails to loosen the kernels from the husks. Then, using a large wooden pitchfork, the workers throw the grain in the air so the wind can blow the chaff, husks, and straw to one side while the heavy kernels fall onto the floor.

Rabbis offer two possible reasons for Boaz staying the night. The great eleventh-century rabbi Rashi says that this was a time of huge societal upheavals and that Boaz was afraid of robbers stealing his grain. Other rabbis comment that if the threshing floor was known to be vacant, courting couples might go there to be away from their parents' watchful eyes.

Ruth's story takes place during the barley harvest and is read in synagogues on Shavuot, a Jewish harvest holiday in late spring. It's also the holiday to commemorate when the

Suddenly the kinsman he had mentioned to Ruth walks by, as Boaz knew he would. Boaz calls out, "Come sit down here!" And his cousin sits down.

Then Boaz invites ten of the elders to sit down as well.

Boaz says to his cousin, "Naomi, who has returned from Moab, is selling a portion of the land that belonged to our kinsman Elimelech." He adds that if his cousin is truly going to buy that land, he should tell the elders gathered there. "For if you will not redeem, tell me . . . for I am after you, and I will redeem."

The cousin seizes the opportunity. "I will redeem it."

Then Boaz points out that if his cousin buys the land, the hand in marriage to Ruth the Moabite woman comes with it. Boaz means that the price for actually buying the land includes supporting both widows—Naomi and Ruth—as well as marrying Ruth in order to father a child who will own the land after him.

His cousin realizes he cannot do all that. He explains by saying, "I might jeopardize my own inheritance." He means that he doesn't have enough money, and it could well bankrupt him. He says to Boaz directly, "You redeem it for yourself, for I cannot redeem it." He removes his sandal and hands it to Boaz.

Delighted, Boaz turns to the ten elders. "You are witnesses today that I

Ten Commandments were given to the Jewish people.

WHY DOES RUTH ASK BOAZ TO SPREAD HIS ROBE OVER HER?

That act is an actual part of an ancient marriage proposal. As kinsman to Ruth's late husband, it's Boaz's duty to find someone closer in kinship than he to marry her or to marry her himself. This is called the "levirate obligation" (Deuteronomy 25:5–10). Naomi has taken a huge chance by sending Ruth uninvited to the threshing ground that night. Boaz could have rejected her or had her thrown out of the village because she's a Moabite.

WHY DOES BOAZ INVITE TEN MEN TO SIT DOWN?

In those days, ten men were considered the necessary number for legally witnessing a business deal. Later on, ten men also became the number needed for a minyan in order to have a full worship service. In some synagogues today, women are counted in a minyan as well.

have bought all of the land that was Elimelech's from Naomi and also have acquired Ruth the Moabite as my wife, in order to preserve the name of the deceased that his name not be obliterated from the tribe."

The witnesses all answer, "We are." And so it is done.

Ruth and Boaz are soon married, and she bears him a son.

The women neighbors tell Naomi about her grandson, "Blessed is the Lord who did not deprive you of a redeemer today, and may his name, Obed, become famous in Israel." And they all add, "Your daughter-in-law who loves you is better to you than seven sons." They also say, "A child is born to Naomi."

That is when Naomi takes up her grandson and holds him to her heart. It is she who looks after him.

The story of Ruth ends with the list of Obed's generations to come, for he is the father of Jesse, and Jesse is the father of David, who becomes Israel's greatest king. That makes Ruth the great-grandmother of King David.

WHAT'S GOING ON WITH THIS MARRIAGE AND THE SANDAL?

The cousin doesn't want to marry a poor immigrant, especially a Moabite. (Presumably he doesn't know she's a convert.) He understands that in a levirate marriage, any child will be considered his dead cousin's child. But Boaz sees the purity, hardworking nature, and kindness of Ruth.

In Israel at that time, a man took off his shoe and handed it to another man to seal a legal transaction, especially in front of witnesses.

HOW CAN NAOMI BE THE GRANDMOTHER?

Ruth's son, Obed, is actually fathered by Boaz, but by the laws of the levirate marriage, the child is also considered to have been fathered by Ruth's late husband, son of Naomi's husband Elimelech. That way Obed will inherit both the land that Naomi owns and Boaz's lands, too.

THIS BIBLE STORY SEEMS DIFFERENT FROM THE OTHERS

It's the only one that "centers around a female-based family struggling for survival in a man's world. It is a story of women's culture and women's values. It is about absolute commitment, embracing connection, and love as a spiritual path" (Raver, p. 147). It is also about how ideals are more important than biology and about how the Jews should, in Raver's words, "accept the dedicated convert as kin" (Raver, p. 149).

Meet Me at the Well

Imagine Naomi

I stood there in the road, my heart tearing apart. I looked at Orpah and Ruth, my sweet widowed daughters-in-law, and wondered what future there would be for them in Bethlehem, my home that I had left so long ago. I knew it would be a difficult journey to make by myself, but how could I expect them to leave Moab, their home?

I stopped at this crossroads and begged them to turn back. They cried. I pleaded. I cried. Finally Orpah kissed me and walked away.

But Ruth did not. Instead Ruth said those unbelievable words to me. "Wherever you go, I will go. Your people will be my people. And your God, my God."

I stood there speechless in front of this tall, sincere, young daughter-in-law of mine. Her eyes looked directly into mine, and I could see her love there.

That is when I knew that my journey home would really be possible with Ruth there to help me.

I made a promise to myself then, and I have remembered it. That I would do all I could to help Ruth have a future in Bethlehem. A promise that she could trust me to be kind and watch out for her welfare as I would for my own. In my misery, Ruth gave me hope. And I would be hers.

Imagine Ruth

I trust my mother-in-law, Naomi, or I would not have followed her here, to this place so foreign to me. She has always shown me kindness, sharing her food, never raising her voice or criticizing, treating her friends as mine, too.

Now Naomi tells me to bathe and put sweet perfumes on my skin, to dress with care, then go to the threshing floor where Boaz will be. It is he who owns the field and has been so kind, making sure I have water to drink and food to eat. Making sure I am safe. He is as kind to me as Naomi is.

But I am fearful of approaching Boaz alone at night in this way. Women do not do this. What will he think of me?

My hands shake as I slip my shawl around my shoulders. Yet I have no doubt that Naomi does only what is best for me. So I will think of her words and not my worries. I will follow her words exactly.

As nervous and fearful as I am, I'm also a little excited. Me, a woman left widowed and childless, approaching a man who sleeps on a threshing floor that he owns. I am thinking Naomi has plans for me and this Boaz. Good plans. But no more thinking just now. Only doing.

My God, Your God

Two women, two women
   on the road.
Two women sharing
   a very heavy load.

         Two women, two widows,
            each once a wife.
         Death is their heavy load,
            as well as life.

   Two women, yes,
share a wrenching grief,
  share a single God
    and a belief.

         So God has lightened
           each heavy load,
           shortened as well
         the hardness of the road.

God has made a sentence
that both women share:
  Your God, my God,
    this I swear.

9

Esther

Queen and Heroine

Of all the parts of the Bible, the Book of Esther (Hadassah) is the one that feels most like a folktale or literary fiction. In it, the most beautiful woman in the kingdom saves her people from a horrible end by putting her own life on the line. It is also the last woman's tale in the Jewish Bible, written when the Jews were in exile from the Holy Land.

Miki Raver writes that Esther is "Persian on the surface and Jewish in her heart" (Raver, p. 160), something to keep in mind as you read the story. The story is also full of courage, hatred, love, risk-taking, and reversals of fortune, all within a foreign setting filled with lots and lots of feasting! Unlike the other sections of the Bible, God isn't mentioned in the Book of Esther. Nor are there any awesome miracles. Instead the plot gets its power and motivations from chance encounters and odd coincidences. The rabbis assumed that God's hand is hidden in the events of the story. The name Esther reflects the Hebrew word nistar, which means "hidden." The Book of Esther also has exaggeration and reversals in its story.

Esther's story is told in ten chapters in Megillat Esther, the Book (or Scroll) of Esther, in the section of the Bible called *The Writings*.

King Ahasuerus of Persia (now Iran), sometimes identified as Xerxes, ruled over a mighty kingdom. In the third year Ahasuerus is king, he decides to invite the officials and courtiers of all the provinces he rules to his magnificent palace in Shushan in order to show them how rich and powerful he is. For one hundred eighty days, the riches of his kingdom are displayed.

At the end of the display, Ahasuerus holds a huge feast lasting seven days in the garden courtyard for all the people of Shushan. There are couches made of gold and silver that stand on the marble and mother-of-pearl floors. Royal wine is served in abundance in gold cups. In fact, the king commands that every man drink as much as he likes.

On the seventh day, merry with wine, the king commands his seven chamberlains to bring Queen Vashti to the men's feast wearing her royal crown to show off her great beauty.

Vashti refuses to go.

Furious, the king calls for his wise men, the ones who know law and judgment. They tell him Vashti has not only wronged him, but also wronged all the princes and all the people (they really mean men) in the king's provinces. The wise men warn, "Vashti's misdeed will encourage other women to challenge their husbands' authority in the home.

SINCE XERXES I WAS A REAL KING, DID THIS ALL REALLY HAPPEN?

Perhaps not. Also, exaggeration is one of the literary techniques of this tale. The Ahasuerus in this story is much less decisive than Xerxes ever was. Greek historian Herodotus, writing around the time that Xerxes reigned, said of the king that he was occasionally principled and wise, but more often he was a tyrant and a brutal despot. Some historians think that the king in the Book of Esther is actually Artaxerxes, who ruled from 405 to 359 BCE and was one of Xerxes's sons. He had even more wives than his father—350 of them!

WHY DOES QUEEN VASHTI REFUSE?

Perhaps Vashti refuses to go when summoned to the men's feast because—as some commentaries have argued—the king asks her to come naked except for her crown. Or perhaps she refuses because she knows her husband is drunk. Or perhaps she refuses because he did not ask politely. All we know from

meet me at the Well

You must put Vashti aside. And let it be written in the laws of Persia and Media that Vashti may never again enter the king's presence. Let the king bestow her royal status on another woman better than she."

And so he does.

The king's servants suggest that all the unmarried and beautiful young women in the kingdom be brought to the harem under the supervision of the harem master Hegai. They will be provided with cosmetics, and the maiden who pleases Ahasuerus the most will become the new queen.

This plan appeals to the king. And here Esther's story begins.

Esther is an orphan who has been raised by Mordecai, her older relative, almost as his own child.

Esther is one of the women selected to enter the king's harem because of her great beauty. There she wins over Hegai's favor with her sweet nature, and he treats her and her maids with special kindness. Esther is given a twelve-month course of beauty treatments to make her ready to meet the king. However, she does not reveal her Jewish religion or her relationship to Mordecai because he has told her not to.

After Esther goes to live in the palace, it becomes Mordecai's custom to walk in front of the court every day to see how she is getting on.

the scroll is that Vashti refuses. Some commentators even think there is a whole hidden history about the relationship between powerful men and women in Vashti's refusal.

WAS QUEEN VASHTI WICKED?

Some commentaries show Vashti in a harsh light, saying she enslaved Jewish women, ordered them to work on the Sabbath, and if they refused, had them beaten, though none of that is in the Bible itself. Some commentators call her vain and controlling. In the nineteenth century, Vashti became a symbol of women's strength to many feminists, including suffragette Elizabeth Cady Stanton and writer Harriet Beecher Stowe, author of Uncle Tom's Cabin.

Vashti disappears from the scroll. Perhaps she is sent back to her original home or returned to the harem—no longer queen. There is midrash that interprets Vashti's disappearance as a death sentence. Indeed, one translation of the Bible says, "Let the king decree that she lose her head."

When King Ahasuerus finally meets Esther, he is so smitten with her that he sets the royal crown on her head and makes her queen. He finishes by throwing a big banquet in her honor.

With Esther on the throne, Mordecai now sits at the royal gate keeping watch on things, listening to what people say about her. One day he overhears two of the chamberlains planning to kill the king.

Mordecai immediately warns Esther, who tells the king what Mordecai has discovered. Ahasuerus orders that the two wicked chamberlains be executed, and Mordecai's name and deed are written into the king's chronicles.

But another kind of plot is brewing. The king's highest counselor, Haman, has long hated Mordecai, who does not treat Haman as special and does not bow down to him, as Haman thinks he should. Haman is so furious that he believes killing Mordecai is not enough. He plots to destroy the people of Mordecai—all the Jews in the entire kingdom of Ahasuerus.

Haman says to the king: "There is a certain people scattered abroad and dispersed among the peoples in all the provinces of your kingdom. Their laws are different from those of every people, neither do they keep the king's laws. It is not in your interest to allow them to stay."

When Haman sees that the king is listening intently, he adds, "If it pleases

WHAT IS ESTHER'S RELATIONSHIP TO MORDECAI?

In the Latin translation of the story, she is called Mordecai's niece. But the Hebrew specifically says she is the daughter of Mordecai's uncle, which would make her his cousin. Their biological relationship is unclear. Esther also has been called Mordecai's ward (like a foster child). The accepted Hebrew version says Mordecai adopted her after her parents' deaths. According to the Aramaic translation of the Bible— Aramaic is an ancient Semitic language—her father died while her mother was pregnant with Esther, and her mother died in childbirth.

WHY DOES ESTHER KEEP HER JEWISHNESS A SECRET?

First because she trusts Mordecai and he tells her to. Second because

the king, let it be written that they be destroyed, and I will pay ten thousand talents of silver for deposit in the royal treasury."

The king gives Haman a special signet ring so that everyone will know Haman has the king's permission to do what he wants.

Haman casts lots (like drawing straws) to set the day of the destruction of the kingdom's Jews. The lot falls on the thirteenth day of the Hebrew month of Adar. Letters bearing the king's seal are sent out to every city, town, and outpost in the kingdom instructing them that on that day all Jews should be killed—every man, woman, and child.

Mordecai discovers this awful plan. He tears his clothes and puts on sackcloth and ashes. He goes through the city crying out loudly and bitterly.

Queen Esther's handmaidens hear of this strange behavior and come to tell her about it. She doesn't understand what Mordecai is doing and sends him fresh clothing, but he refuses it and sends it back to her without explaining the problem. At that point, Esther sends out Hathach, one of the chamberlains loyal to her, to find out what is going on.

Hathach speaks to Mordecai and is told the entire plot. Mordecai even hands Hathach a copy of the decree with the king's own seal, instructing Hathach to take it to Esther. He asks Hathach to tell her that she must go to Ahasuerus and plead for their people.

even though most Persian rulers at that time were tolerant of the various ethnic and cultural groups in the kingdom, being a Jew might have lessened Esther's chances of becoming queen. At that time the Jews were especially known to strictly follow their own religious and cultural rules instead of following the king's.

How Old Is Esther When She Marries the King?

In the story Esther seems quite young, but one rabbinical commentary insists that as one of the four most beautiful women ever created, she remained eternally young and puts her age at around forty when she married Ahasuerus. Some commentaries even guess that she's in her seventies, as calculated by the numerical value of the letters in Hadassah, her Hebrew name.

But going in to see the king without being invited is an executable offense. If any person dares to enter the king's presence in the inner court without first being summoned, that person will be put to death. Only if the king extends the golden scepter to that person will he or she be spared.

Esther tells Mordecai via her messenger, "I have not been called to come in unto the king these thirty days."

Mordecai reminds her, "Do not think that by being in the king's house you, more than any other Jew, will escape."

Knowing he is right, Esther realizes she must risk approaching the king. As Mordecai tells her, "Perhaps for a time such as this you have become part of royalty."

Esther's final note to Mordecai says: "Go gather together all the Jews who are in Shushan, and fast for me for three days. Don't eat or drink during the day or night. My attendants and I will fast as well. Afterward, although it is against the law, I will go to the king. If I perish, I perish."

Mordecai does as she asks.

On the third day of the fast—terrified, but ready for her ordeal—Esther dons her most flattering royal clothes. She goes to the inner court of the king's house, even though he has not sent for her.

King Ahasuerus sees her there,

HOW IS HAMAN ABLE TO PLOT AGAINST THE JEWS?

Haman was related to the Amalekites, an ancient enemy of Israel. Haman doesn't tell the king the people he is talking about are Jews. Also, he doesn't know that Esther, the king's beloved queen, is Jewish. He offers to pay a huge sum to the king's treasury to make this genocide happen. The king seems to let Haman have his way. Or at least he doesn't question Haman much about it. If this reminds you of Hitler and the planned destruction of all the Jews in Europe (Hitler orchestrated the killing of six million Jews), you might be interested to know that Hitler banned the reading of the Book of Esther because the Jews win in the end. Hitler called it "a pack of Jewish lies."

WHY DOES ESTHER HESITATE?

Esther's statement suggests that she may have lost favor with the king.

looking radiant. He holds out the golden scepter toward her, giving her permission to join him. She walks toward him and touches the top of the scepter.

"What troubles you, Queen Esther?" the king asks. "For whatever you request, even to half my kingdom, it shall be given you."

She answers, "If it seems good unto the king, let the king and Haman come this day to a banquet that I have prepared."

Turning to his chamberlain, Ahasuerus orders him to tell Haman to do as the queen requests.

Thinking this a great honor, Haman hurries to the feast. When they are sitting over their wine, the king asks Esther again what she wants, adding as he did before, "Whatever you request, even to half my kingdom, it shall be given you."

Smiling, she answers, "If I have found favor in your sight, I wish that you and Haman come to the banquet I shall prepare tomorrow and at that banquet I will do as the king asks." She means that she will make her actual request at the second banquet. Haman is enjoying being invited to all these feasts.

Full of pride that he has been so honored twice, Haman goes out of the gate happily. But there he sees Mordecai again and, when Mordecai does not rise or show any sign of respect, Haman is filled with rage. On his return home, he tells his wife, Zeresh, and his friends

Perhaps he no longer loves her. Perhaps he will have her killed. Maybe she remembers what happened to Vashti, who disobeyed the king, and that is why she is afraid. The Bible doesn't tell us directly, though there is plenty of speculation in commentaries.

WHY DOES ESTHER ASK THE JEWS TO FAST FOR THREE DAYS?

Perhaps everyone fasted with Esther in solidarity with her. It was a way they could show how much they cared for her. Also it was a way to let God know they wanted Esther to succeed. Or perhaps the Jews, afraid of their own destruction, were already in mourning for what might happen. It seems that this story is purposely exaggerated for effect, especially where food and feasts are concerned, which could account for the three days of fasting. Or maybe the three days was a local custom. The Bible doesn't tell us directly.

how well the king has treated him, better than any prince. He says it means nothing to him as long as the Jew Mordecai has once again treated him disrespectfully. Zeresh counsels him: "Make a gallows fifty cubits high, and in the morning speak to the king that Mordecai might be hanged there, and then merrily go in with the king to the queen's banquet."

This idea so pleases Haman that he plans to do that very thing.

Now the night before the second banquet, King Ahasuerus can't sleep. He commands his servant to bring him the great book of records so they may be read aloud to him.

The servant opens the Chronicles and begins reading. He comes to the part where Mordecai saves the king's life by overhearing the treason plotted by the two chamberlains.

The king asks, "What honor has been done to Mordecai for this?" And when he is told that nothing was done, Ahasuerus asks who is in the court at that early hour.

It so happens that Haman is there, waiting to speak to the king about hanging Mordecai on the gallows he has just had built. The king sends for him.

Haman arrives and without preamble the king asks, "What shall be done unto a man the king wishes to honor?"

Of course, Haman thinks the king means him, and says, "For such a man let royal apparel be brought which the king himself wears and the horse the king rides on, and let there be a royal crown on the horse's head. And let that apparel and horse be delivered to

---

IS THERE MIDRASH ABOUT ESTHER IN WHICH GOD OR ANGELS PLAY A PART?

There's a tale: Aware of her danger, Esther prayed and God answered her petition by sending three angels. One enveloped her face with "the threads of grace," the second raised her head, and the third drew out the scepter of Ahasuerus until it touched her.

The king looked away, to avoid seeing Esther, but the angels forced him to look at her and he was conquered by her charm (Ginzberg, "Esther").

the hand of one of the king's most noble princes who will put the man on the horse in his finery, and the prince shall walk in front leading the horse through the city, proclaiming, 'Thus shall it be done to a man whom the king wishes to honor.'"

King Ahasuerus nods, saying, "Get the robe and horse as you have said. And do this for Mordecai the Jew who sits in the royal gate. Leave nothing out of what you have said."

What can Haman do but follow these direct orders? How can he mention the gallows? He leads Mordecai around on the king's horse, seething as he does so. Afterward, he goes home, grieving, hoping his wife and friends will help him. But instead, they tell him, "If Mordecai before whom you are beginning to fall is a Jew, you cannot win against him. You will surely be brought down."

They are still discussing this when the chamberlains arrive to bring Haman into the second banquet that Esther has prepared. There once again Ahasuerus asks Esther what it is she wants.

Has King Ahasuerus Changed?

We don't really know. Ahasuerus demonstrably had problems with Queen Vashti, who proved to be a strong woman. Yet now he seems to be doing everything Queen Esther asks of him. Perhaps he has changed. Perhaps he loves Esther more than he'd ever loved his first queen. Perhaps Esther asks for things in a way that makes the king seem strong and generous, while Vashti offended him by challenging him in front of all the other princes. But none of that is stated outright in the Book of Esther.

Esther says, "If I have found favor in your sight, O king, and if it pleases the king, let my life be given me at my petition, and my people at my request." She adds, "I and my people are to be destroyed, to be slain, and to perish. If we had only been sold for bondmen and bondwomen, I would have held my peace."

The king demands answers, asking Queen Esther, "Who is he, and where is he, that dare presume in his heart to do so?"

Esther answers, "An adversary and an enemy, is this wicked Haman."

Imagine her pointing a finger at Haman, who trembles in terror at her words. This is the first time Haman learns Esther is Jewish.

The king is so angry that he leaves the table and goes into the garden.

The minute the king leaves, Haman flings himself on the queen's couch to beg for mercy. He still doesn't know that her cousin is Mordecai. Perhaps he believes he can convince her it is all some awful mistake.

But at that moment the king returns, and he sees Haman on his wife's couch. He roars, "Will you even ravish the queen before me in my own house?"

If Haman's fate had not yet been sealed, it is now. And when the chamberlain Harbonah comes in and tells the king of the gallows Haman has built to hang the hero, Mordecai, King Ahasuerus does not hesitate.

"Hang Haman thereon," he says.

And it is done.

Only now does Esther reveal how Mordecai is related to her, and Mordecai presents himself to the king.

However there is still a problem. Haman's original letter to all governors and princes of the realm has been sealed with the king's ring, which makes it irreversible. Esther pleads with the king again, falling at his feet and weeping. So the king gives Mordecai the ring he took back from Haman and

> ### AREN'T THERE A LOT OF PARTIES IN THE BOOK OF ESTHER?
>
> *The word for banquet (mishteh) occurs forty-six times in the Bible, twenty of them in the Book of Esther! The king holds not one but two very long feasts at the beginning of the narrative. Then, at Esther's crowning, there is another royal banquet. Esther and Mordecai's plot unfolds at two small, private dinners. Finally the story comes to the feast of Purim, the celebration of the deliverance of the Jews from Haman's wicked schemes. That's a lot of eating!*

tells Esther and Mordecai to write a *new* letter, also sealed with his ring, granting the Jews in every city and town the right to arm themselves on the day of the intended slaughter, the thirteenth day of the twelfth month of Adar.

Copies of the letter go by the swiftest of horses. And because Mordecai has been raised so high in the king's court, and Esther remains the king's most beloved queen, not many people dare stand against the Jews on the appointed day. Those who do are killed, including Haman's sons. The next day the Jews rest and hold a feast day.

From Ahasuerus's time forward, Jews have celebrated the anniversary with a day of feasting known as Purim, a time that was transformed from one of grief and mourning to one of gladness and joy. There are costumes and games, plays, feasts, and laughter, and the sending of gifts of food to one another and presents to the poor.

WHY IS THIS HOLIDAY DIFFERENT FROM OTHER JEWISH HOLIDAYS?

It is seemingly a very secular holiday, almost like a carnival, where people dress up, wear masks, are allowed to drink too much, act silly, and loudly boo and shake noisemakers at every mention of the villain Haman's name. The good humor reminds us of how the story is about the powerful reversals of fortune—one queen is thrown down, while another rises up. The entire Jewish community is threatened and saved. Mordecai is to be hanged, but his enemy Haman is hanged instead, on the very gallows erected for Mordecai. Reversals.

Over the centuries rabbis and scholars have debated whether the festival is Jewish or instead based on a Persian New Year celebration. Yet the holiday reflects the twin themes of Jewish escape from the direst peril (again!) and God's hidden hand in all that transpires.

Imagine Esther

I am told I am beautiful, especially here in the king's palace. But growing up with Mordecai—my father and mother put together—I knew myself more as a sweeper of floors, kneader of bread, feeder of chickens, giver of alms to the poor.

Here I bathe daily in perfumed oils, have lotions rubbed on my skin, am served by seven maids and Hegai, who bring me whatever I wish.

It is strange, these two lives of mine.

But Mordecai says this has all happened to me for a reason. It will be clear in time why I have been picked to be part of this pageant of beauties, one of whom will be chosen as Queen. The one who most pleases the King—this man I have never seen, but hear many tales about.

Mordecai says I must be brave.

Whenever I can, I find a spot by the window and look for Mordecai, who comes every day for news about me.

I am by the window now and see his beloved face down below in the courtyard. Of course, we cannot talk, but just looking at him fills me with relief and courage. He is the link between my old world and this new one.

I try not to forget who I am, a Jewess, though I have not told anyone in the palace that fact. I am careful what I eat here, selecting lentils instead of lamb, and celebrating the Sabbath as I can.

Mordecai says I must be brave.

We send messages to each other through Hegai, the guardian of the women in the palace. And I wait to be presented to the king. Waiting to be chosen queen? From among all these beauties? Will I ever?

My old friends would not believe me, but I sometimes miss being a feeder of chickens and kneader of bread.

Two Queens

Straighten back, bend no knee,
look your ruler in the eye,
wear the purple robes of power,
head held high, held high.

Sweet perfume, attar of roses,
hiding stench of awful fear.
Bend no knee, head held high,
the king is here, is here.

Get the promise, absolution,
face all those who wish you ill.
Wear the purple robes of power,
you're here still, here still.

A Parting Note from the Authors

This is the end, but it's a beginning, too. Now you have read about these fourteen strong, brave, fascinating girls and women of the Bible and their often-hidden lives. You have contemplated the responses that have come from centuries—millennia, even—of readers who have wrestled with the meanings of these stories. You have story-walked in their shoes.

With our sidebars and marginalia, our imagine pieces and poems, we have offered you additional road maps for your walk.

It is time for you to add to these centuries-long conversations. Discuss these girls and women and their stories with your friends, parents, or teachers. Wherever you come from and wherever you are going, we think that you will surely have responses to what you've read here. Those responses may include questions, arguments, or even amazement. You might ask: *Why have I not heard this before? What were these women thinking? Would I have acted differently from them?* Any response you have is part of a deeper understanding, part of growing, and part of finding your own place in the world.

We encourage you to speak, write, or pass on your thoughts to others. And when you think about these girls and women, and talk about their accomplishments, you will be making *midrashim*.

About the Authors

Barbara's family celebrated the Jewish holidays with enthusiasm and with a table always laden with the delicious traditional foods of the holiday. (Yes, her mom's matzah balls always floated!) She attended Hebrew school after her public-school classes and graduated from Gratz Hebrew High School in Philadelphia. She became a bar- and bat-mitzvah tutor, taught in a synagogue preschool, and then later taught English and creative writing at a Jewish day school.

Barbara has written many books with Jewish themes, and in 1997 received the Sydney Taylor Body-of-Work Award from the Association of Jewish Libraries. The award is presented "to the author whose collected works are a distinguished contribution to Jewish literature for children." Barbara's books include *The World's Birthday: A Rosh Hashanah Story; Cakes and Miracles: A Purim Tale; A Mountain of Blintzes;* and *Journeys with Elijah: Eight Tales of the Prophet.*

On the other hand, Jane did not attend synagogue on a regular basis until she was thirteen. Her household was not kosher, nor were the holidays celebrated except when her family went to visit relatives. However, when Jane was thirteen, she asked her parents to let her be confirmed. (Bat-mitzvah ceremonies were hardly known then.) Her parents had to join a temple for as long as it took for confirmation study—a little over a year. She learned to read Hebrew, was the first girl in the history of that particular Reform temple to read from the Torah, and then went on to minor in religion at college.

Jane has written a number of books with Jewish themes, most notably two Holocaust novels: *The Devil's Arithmetic* and *Briar Rose.* She also wrote the folktale cookbook *Jewish Fairy Tale Feasts,* the book of poems *O Jerusalem,* and a recent Holocaust picture book, *Stone Angel.* She won the Sydney Taylor Book Award and a National Jewish Book Award for *The Devil's Arithmetic* (made into a movie starring Kirsten Dunst) and a Sydney Taylor Honor for *Naming Liberty.*

Bibliography

Books, Writing, and Websites Cited

Cohen, Gabriel. "Rachel and Leah—Wife and Mother." Lecture, Bar-Ilan University, Tel Aviv, Israel, December 10, 2005. http://www.biu.ac.il/JH/Parasha/eng/vayetze/koh.html.

Frankel, Ellen. *The Classic Tales: 4,000 Years of Jewish Lore*. Northvale, NJ: Jason Aronson, 1989.

———. *The Five Books of Miriam: A Woman's Commentary on the Torah*. Reprint ed. New York: HarperOne, 1997.

Frymer-Kensky, Tikva. *Reading the Women of the Bible: A New Interpretation of Their Stories*. New York: Schocken, 2002.

Ginzberg, Louis. *The Legend of the Jews*. 7 vols. Philadelphia: Jewish Publication Society of America, 1988. First published 1909. http://www.sacred-texts.com/jud/loj/.

Keller, Werner. *The Bible as History: Archaeology Confirms the Book of Books*. London: Hodder & Stoughton, 1957.

Klapholtz, Yisroel Y. *A Treasury of Torah Aggados*. Brooklyn, NY: Mishor, 2006.

Lieber, David L., ed. *Etz Hayim: Torah and Commentary*. New York: Jewish Publication Society, 2001.

My Jewish Learning staff. "Sarah and the Akedah." *My Jewish Learning* website. http://www.myjewishlearning.com/article/sarah-and-the-akedah/2/.

Orlinsky, Harry M., et al., eds. *Tanakh: A New Translation of the Holy Scriptures According to the Traditional Hebrew Text*. Philadelphia: Jewish Publication Society, 1985.

Pearce, Rabbi Stephen. "Haye Sarah: Seeing Isaac's Weaknesses and Strengths." *Jewish Weekly*, November 17, 1995. http://www.jweekly.com/article/full/1988/haye-sarah-seeing-isaac-s-weaknesses-and-strengths/.

meet me at the well

Plaskow, Judith. "The Coming of Lilith." Jewish Women's Archive website. https://www.jwa.org/media/coming-of-lilith-by-judith-plaskow.

Plaut, W. Gunther. *The Torah: A Modern Commentary*. Revised ed. New York: Union of American Hebrew Congregations, 1981.

Raver, Miki. *Listen to Her Voice: Women of the Hebrew Bible*. San Francisco: Chronicle, 2005.

Scherman, Rabbi Nosson. *The Chumash: The Stone Edition*. Brooklyn, NY: Mesorah, 2000.

Shachter, Jacob, and H. Freedman, trans., and Rabbi I. Epstein, ed. *Babylonian Talmud: Tractate Sanhedrin*. http://www.come-and-hear.com/sanhedrin/sanhedrin_39.html.

Simon, Solomon, and Morrison David Bial. *The Rabbis' Bible*. Vol. 1, *Torah*. New York: Behrman House, 1966.

Skolnick, Fred, ed. *Encyclopedia Judaica*. 2nd ed. 22 vols. Farmington Hills, MI: Macmillan Reference USA, 2007.

Steinsaltz, Adin. *Biblical Images: Men and Women of the Book*. New York: Basic, 1984.

United Church of God. "Bible Commentary: Bringing in the Sheaves (Ruth 2)." Beyond Today, United Church of God website. http://bible.ucg.org/bible-commentary/Ruth/Boaz-meets-Ruth-in-his-fields/.

Williams, Michael E., ed. *The Storyteller's Companion to the Bible*. Vol. 2, *Exodus–Joshua*. Nashville, TN: Abingdon, 1992.

Other Books Consulted and for Further Reading

Ackerman, Susan. *Warrior, Dancer, Seductress, Queen: Women in Judges and Biblical Israel*. New York: Doubleday, 1998.

Ali, Abdullah Yusuf. *The Meaning of the Holy Qur'an*. 11th ed. Beltsville, MD: Amana, 2004.

Ausubel, Nathan, ed. *A Treasury of Jewish Folklore: Stories, Traditions, Legends, Humor, Wisdom, and Folk Songs of the Jewish People*. New York: Crown, 1989.

Brenner, Athalya, ed. *A Feminist Companion to Genesis*. 2nd ed. Sheffield, England: Sheffield Academic Press, 1993.

Brockington, L. H. *Ezra, Nehemiah and Esther*. Century Bible. London: Thomas Nelson, 1969.

Darr, Katheryn Pfisterer. *Far More Precious Than Jewels: Perspectives on Biblical Women*. Louisville, KY: Westminster/John Knox, 1991.

Fox, Michael V. *Character and Ideology in the Book of Esther*. Grand Rapids, MI: Eerdmans, 2001.

Fuerst, Wesley J. *The Books of Ruth, Esther, Ecclesiastes, the Song of Songs, Lamentations: The Five Scrolls*. Cambridge, England: Cambridge University Press, 1975.

Goldin, Barbara Diamond. *A Family Book of Midrash: 52 Jewish Stories from the Sages*. Northvale, NJ: Jason Aronson, 1996.

Graves, Robert, and Raphael Patai. *Hebrew Myths: The Book of Genesis*. Garden City, NY: Doubleday, 1964.

Hertz, Dr. J. H., ed. *Pentateuch and Haftorahs*. 2nd ed. London: Soncino, 1960.

Kam, Rose Sallberg. *Their Stories, Our Stories: Women of the Bible*. New York: Continuum, 1995.

Kravitz, Leonard S., and Kerry M. Olitzky, trans. *Esther: A Modern Commentary*. New York: URJ, 2010.

Matthews, Victor H. *Judges and Ruth*. Cambridge, England: Cambridge University Press, 2004.

Noy, Dov, ed. *Folktales of Israel*. Chicago: University of Chicago Press, 1963.

Rush, Barbara. *The Book of Jewish Women's Tales*. Northvale, NJ: Jason Aronson, 1994.

Sasson, Jack M. *Ruth: A New Translation with a Philological Commentary and Formalist-Folklorist Interpretation*. Baltimore, MD: Johns Hopkins University Press, 1979.

Schley, Donald G., ed. *Shiloh: A Biblical City in Tradition and History*. Sheffield, England: Sheffield Academic Press, 2009.

Schwartz, Howard. *Tree of Souls: The Mythology of Judaism*. Oxford, England: Oxford University Press, 2004.

Wolkstein, Diane. *Esther's Story*. New York: HarperCollins, 1996.

Index